Sam Garcia

This book was made possible through
the generous assistance of:

Kodak Eastman Kodak Co.

BankAmerica Corporation

HYATT REGENCY SAN FRANCISCO

UNITED AIRLINES

MCI

Hertz

California Department of Commerce

5:30 AM: As dawn breaks on the morning of Friday, April 29th, a team of longshoremen muscle a one-ton whaling dory by the Port of Oakland.

6:30 AM: Santa Cruz midwife Mary Randick and her three children spend a few minutes playing together before starting their day.

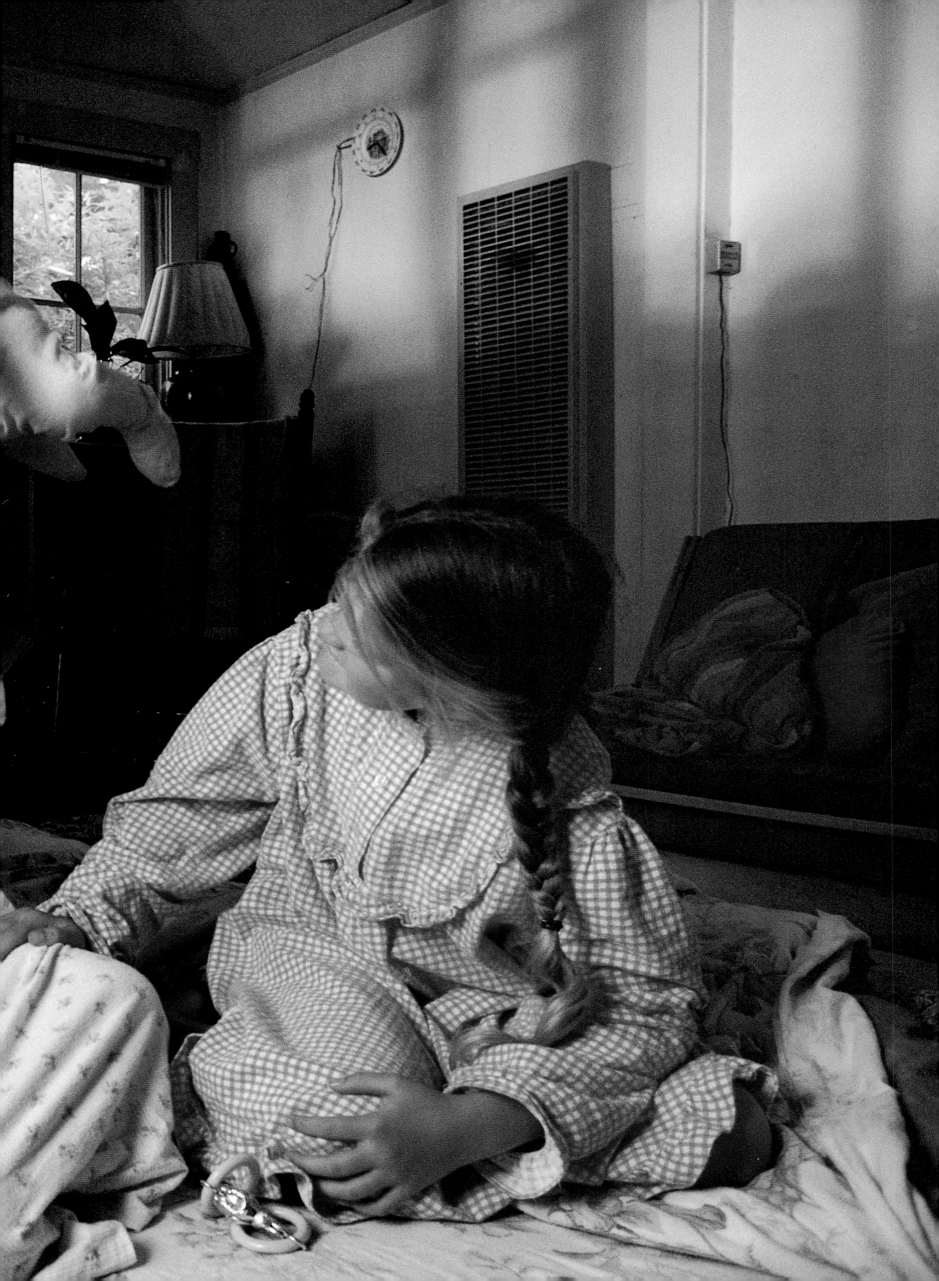

Galen Rowell

First published in 1988 by Collins Publishers, Inc., San Francisco.

Copyright © 1988 by Collins Publishers, Inc.

ISBN 0-00-215163-4

Library of Congress Cataloging-in-Publication Data
Main entry under title: A Day in the Life of California

1. California—Description and travel—1981—Views
2. California—Social life and customs—Pictorial works.
I. Smolan, Rick
II. Cohen, David, 1955-

F862.D38 1988
979.4'053'0222   88-20399

Project Directors: Rick Smolan and David Cohen
Art Director: Jennifer Barry

Printed in Japan
First printing October 1988

10 9 8 7 6 5 4 3 2

A Day in the Life of California

Photographed by 100 of the
world's leading photojournalists
on one day, April 29, 1988

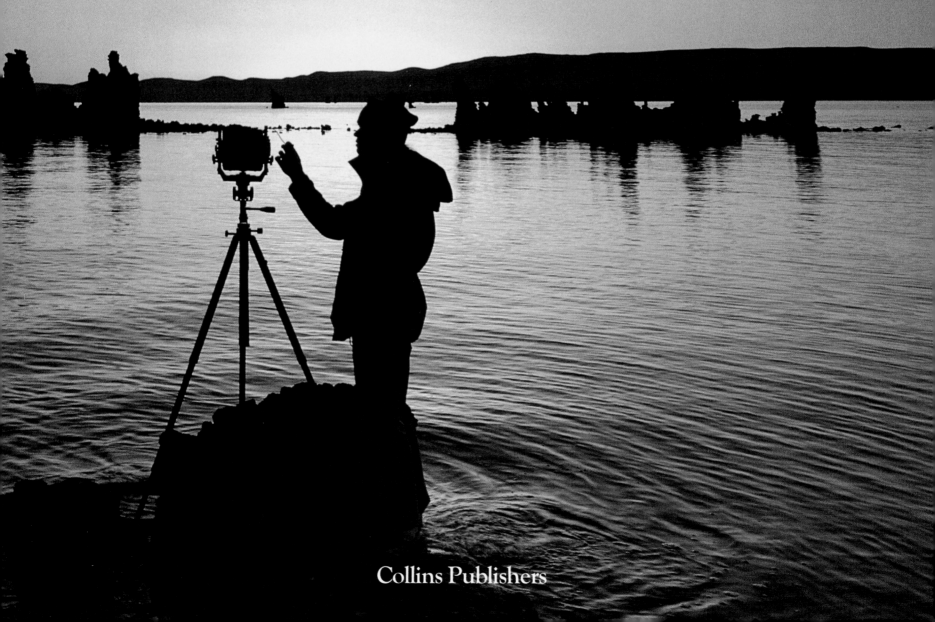

Collins Publishers

7:00 AM: Digger the dog watches his human companion,
Mike Mulrane, shave in the early morning light at the
Sweetwater Mine outside Mariposa.

Hiroshi Suga

When Spanish conquistadors first sighted the golden hills of the Coastal Range they thought they had discovered "an island called California, very near to the Terrestrial Paradise." Their geography was imperfect, but the land they later colonized was undeniably blessed.

On April 29th, 1988, 100 of the world's leading photographers descended on California to capture *A Day in the Life of California*. Those expecting to find a laid-back lifestyle revolving around hot tubs and health spas were not disappointed. Neither were those assigned to photograph America's most productive agricultural state, or the Southern California megalopolis that powers the seventh largest economy in the world.

California today is 20th century America's Ellis Island. One out of every four immigrants entering the United States eventually settles in California. The Mexican population of Los Angeles county is exceeded only by that of Mexico City. Seventy percent of all Asians now living in the continental United States call California home.

The promise of California, and the opportunity it offers newcomers, is not an illusion. Traveling from the fantasy factories of Hollywood to the dense forests near the Oregon border, the *Day in the Life* team found America's most populous state to be as rich in contrasts as it is in superlatives. From gene-splicing to gurus; at baseball stadiums and on beaches, in one action-packed day they encountered a state and a state of mind, peopled by immigrants in search of a new beginning, actors awaiting their big break and others simply following the sun.

This unusual one-day odyssey through California, the state Howard Hughes wanted to develop and John Muir tried to preserve, produced more than 115,000 photographs. As you page through this book remember that no picture here is more than 24 hours older or younger than any other, and no picture was taken for any purpose other than to document the harmonies and paradoxes of life in California as it was lived on this one ordinary day.

— David DeVoss

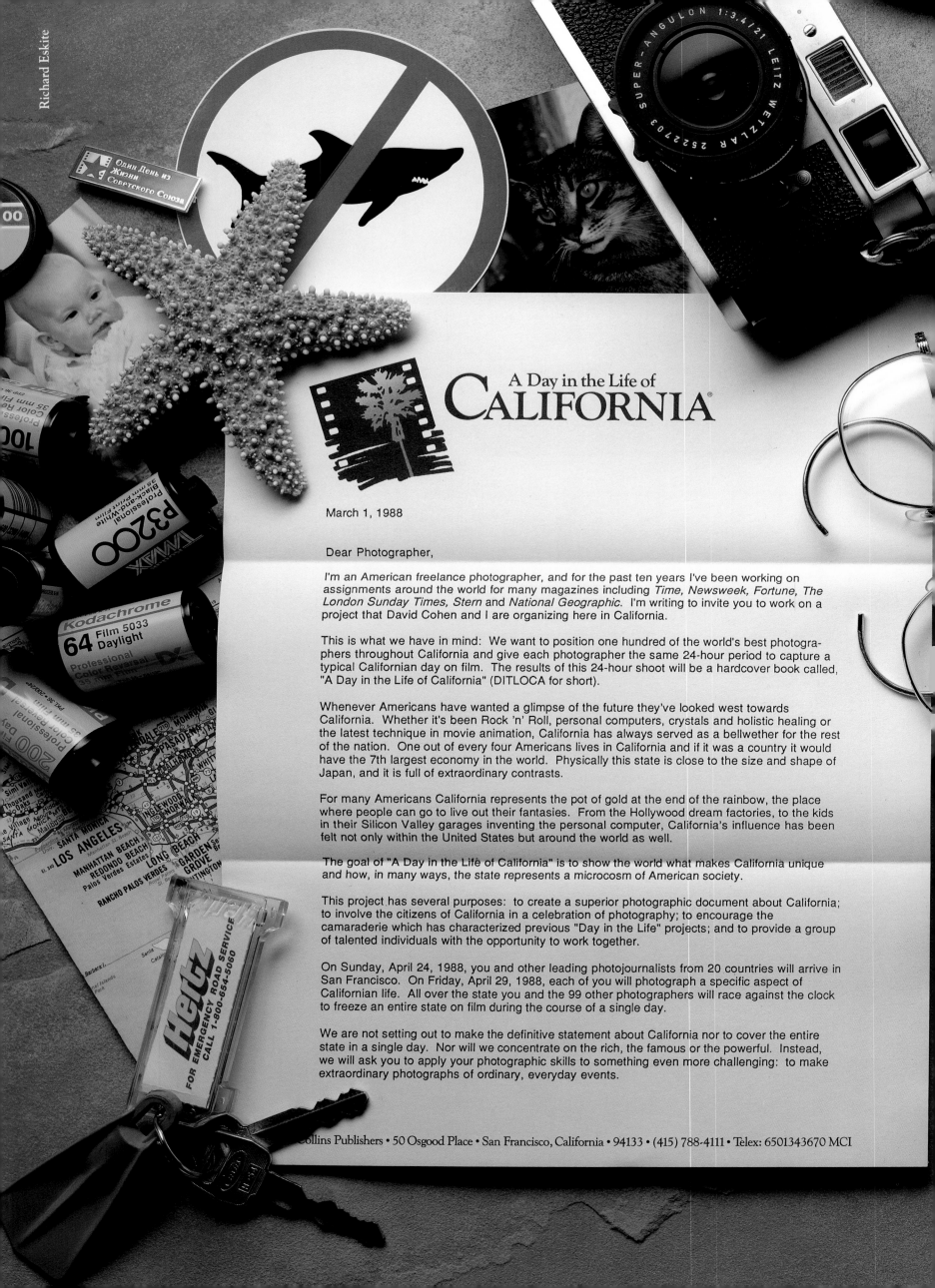

A Day in the Life of CALIFORNIA

March 1, 1988

Dear Photographer,

I'm an American freelance photographer, and for the past ten years I've been working on assignments around the world for many magazines including *Time, Newsweek, Fortune, The London Sunday Times, Stern* and *National Geographic*. I'm writing to invite you to work on a project that David Cohen and I are organizing here in California.

This is what we have in mind: We want to position one hundred of the world's best photographers throughout California and give each photographer the same 24-hour period to capture a typical Californian day on film. The results of this 24-hour shoot will be a hardcover book called, "A Day in the Life of California" (DITLOCA for short).

Whenever Americans have wanted a glimpse of the future they've looked west towards California. Whether it's been Rock 'n' Roll, personal computers, crystals and holistic healing or the latest technique in movie animation, California has always served as a bellwether for the rest of the nation. One out of every four Americans lives in California and if it was a country it would have the 7th largest economy in the world. Physically this state is close to the size and shape of Japan, and it is full of extraordinary contrasts.

For many Americans California represents the pot of gold at the end of the rainbow, the place where people can go to live out their fantasies. From the Hollywood dream factories, to the kids in their Silicon Valley garages inventing the personal computer, California's influence has been felt not only within the United States but around the world as well.

The goal of "A Day in the Life of California" is to show the world what makes California unique and how, in many ways, the state represents a microcosm of American society.

This project has several purposes: to create a superior photographic document about California; to involve the citizens of California in a celebration of photography; to encourage the camaraderie which has characterized previous "Day in the Life" projects; and to provide a group of talented individuals with the opportunity to work together.

On Sunday, April 24, 1988, you and other leading photojournalists from 20 countries will arrive in San Francisco. On Friday, April 29, 1988, each of you will photograph a specific aspect of Californian life. All over the state you and the 99 other photographers will race against the clock to freeze an entire state on film during the course of a single day.

We are not setting out to make the definitive statement about California nor to cover the entire state in a single day. Nor will we concentrate on the rich, the famous or the powerful. Instead, we will ask you to apply your photographic skills to something even more challenging: to make extraordinary photographs of ordinary, everyday events.

Collins Publishers • 50 Osgood Place • San Francisco, California • 94133 • (415) 788-4111 • Telex: 6501343670 MCI

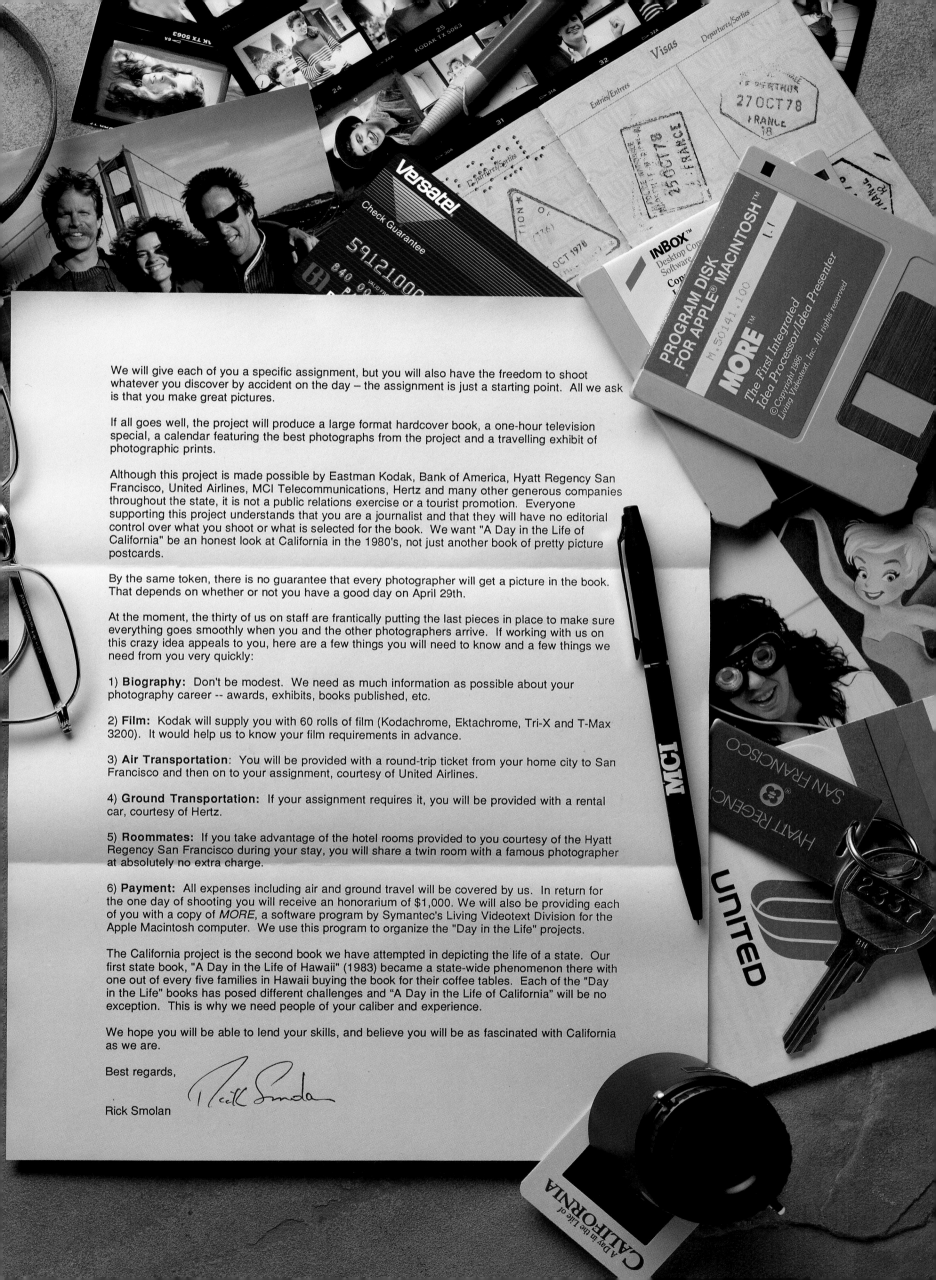

We will give each of you a specific assignment, but you will also have the freedom to shoot whatever you discover by accident on the day – the assignment is just a starting point. All we ask is that you make great pictures.

If all goes well, the project will produce a large format hardcover book, a one-hour television special, a calendar featuring the best photographs from the project and a travelling exhibit of photographic prints.

Although this project is made possible by Eastman Kodak, Bank of America, Hyatt Regency San Francisco, United Airlines, MCI Telecommunications, Hertz and many other generous companies throughout the state, it is not a public relations exercise or a tourist promotion. Everyone supporting this project understands that you are a journalist and that they will have no editorial control over what you shoot or what is selected for the book. We want "A Day in the Life of California" be an honest look at California in the 1980's, not just another book of pretty picture postcards.

By the same token, there is no guarantee that every photographer will get a picture in the book. That depends on whether or not you have a good day on April 29th.

At the moment, the thirty of us on staff are frantically putting the last pieces in place to make sure everything goes smoothly when you and the other photographers arrive. If working with us on this crazy idea appeals to you, here are a few things you will need to know and a few things we need from you very quickly:

1) **Biography:** Don't be modest. We need as much information as possible about your photography career -- awards, exhibits, books published, etc.

2) **Film:** Kodak will supply you with 60 rolls of film (Kodachrome, Ektachrome, Tri-X and T-Max 3200). It would help us to know your film requirements in advance.

3) **Air Transportation**: You will be provided with a round-trip ticket from your home city to San Francisco and then on to your assignment, courtesy of United Airlines.

4) **Ground Transportation:** If your assignment requires it, you will be provided with a rental car, courtesy of Hertz.

5) **Roommates:** If you take advantage of the hotel rooms provided to you courtesy of the Hyatt Regency San Francisco during your stay, you will share a twin room with a famous photographer at absolutely no extra charge.

6) **Payment:** All expenses including air and ground travel will be covered by us. In return for the one day of shooting you will receive an honorarium of $1,000. We will also be providing each of you with a copy of *MORE*, a software program by Symantec's Living Videotext Division for the Apple Macintosh computer. We use this program to organize the "Day in the Life" projects.

The California project is the second book we have attempted in depicting the life of a state. Our first state book, "A Day in the Life of Hawaii" (1983) became a state-wide phenomenon there with one out of every five families in Hawaii buying the book for their coffee tables. Each of the "Day in the Life" books has posed different challenges and "A Day in the Life of California" will be no exception. This is why we need people of your caliber and experience.

We hope you will be able to lend your skills, and believe you will be as fascinated with California as we are.

Best regards,

Rick Smolan

● *Left*

The Bay Bridge links San Francisco and Oakland, the state's third- and sixth-largest cities. Completed in 1936 to accommodate a combination of rail and vehicular traffic, the bridge was converted in 1958 to handle vehicles only. Now the 260,000 cars that cross it each day often .approach gridlock—especially after an early morning rainstorm.
Photographer:
Rick Smolan

● *Above*

Work in progress: For Bernadette Henry of Fremont, getting ready for work is an ongoing process that continues even while waiting for the BART (Bay Area Rapid Transit) train to San Francisco.
Photographer:
Cheryl Nuss

● *Following page*

Starlet: Ron and Carla Finnerman of Los Angeles capture daughter Shannon's first days in the nursery.
Photographer:
Dana Fineman

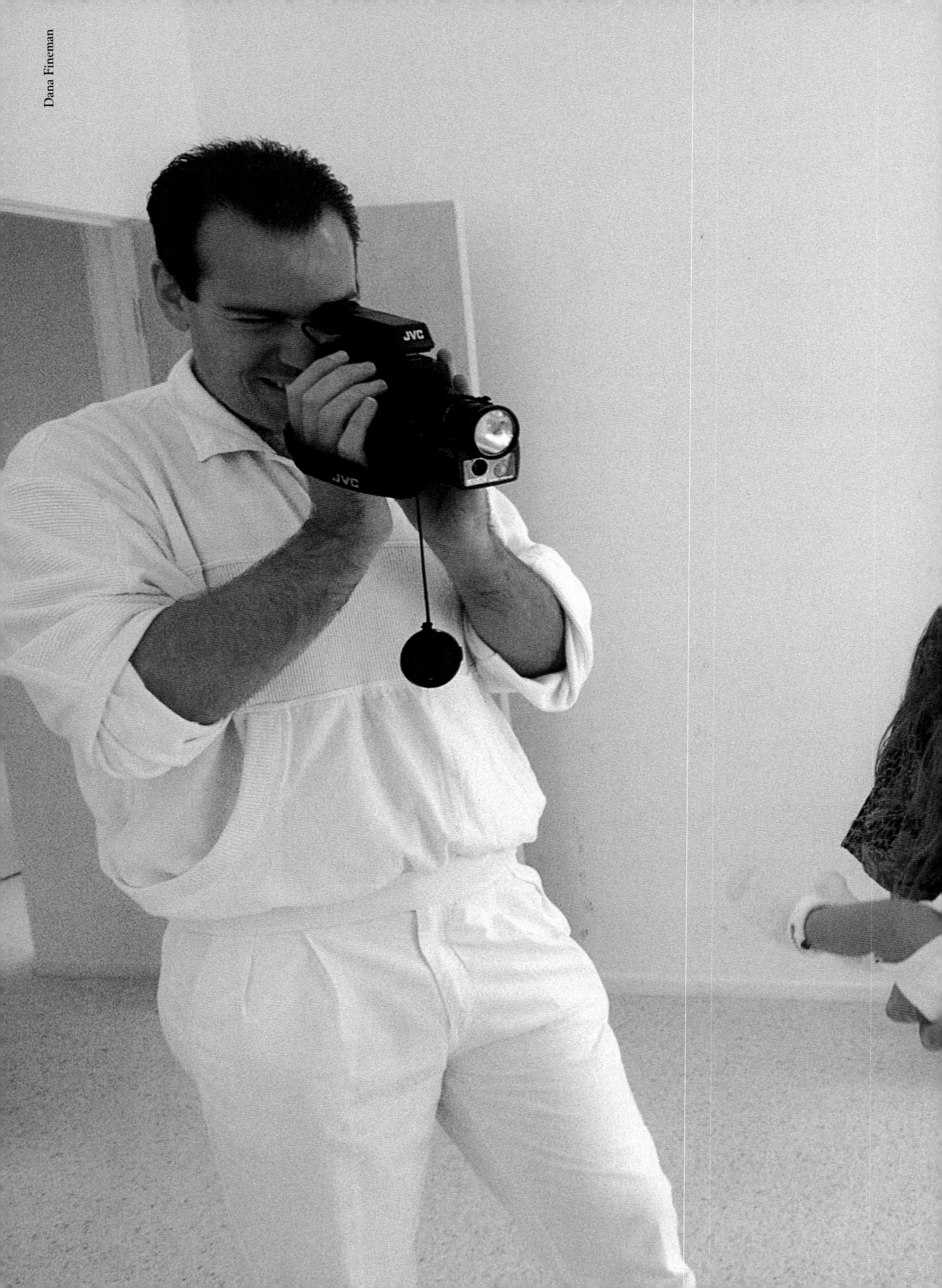

Dana Fineman

● *Above*

Allen Dowling, age 5, is a man with responsibilities. Early each morning he feeds the chickens, cleans out the barn and milks the cows.
Photographer:
Joe Rossi

● *Right*

There have been Dowlings living in Northern California's Scott Valley since 1865. Bernard and Beverly Dowling carry on the family's ranching heritage. Their 12-hour work days begin in the kitchen, where baby Paul watches his mother make breakfast.
Photographer:
Joe Rossi

● *Left*

Carol and Dan Blumberg of San Diego have just moved into their first home. The average cost of a house in this southern city exceeds $160,000.
Photographer:
Joy Wolf

● *Below*

Christopher Gill is a professional masseur who travels the streets of Los Angeles trading rubdowns for food, lodging and other amenities. Gill has massaged his way across the country several times, and has even bartered for airplane tickets. Bill Fischler, who owns Patrick's Roadhouse in Santa Monica, has agreed to trade breakfast for a head and neck rub.
Photographer:
Patrick Downs

● *Above*

David Erwitt and his 4-year-old son, Erik, pick up their mail in Two Harbors. This tiny community (population 75) on the west side of Santa Catalina Island is part of densely populated Los Angeles County (8.8 million), but the Erwitt family feels like it's hundreds of miles away. (In fact, the island is 20 miles off the mainland.) "It's a beautiful, crime-free place," says David, "the perfect place to raise children."

Photographer:
Misha Erwitt

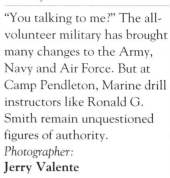

● *Far left*

"You talking to me?" The all-volunteer military has brought many changes to the Army, Navy and Air Force. But at Camp Pendleton, Marine drill instructors like Ronald G. Smith remain unquestioned figures of authority.
Photographer:
Jerry Valente

The prices may be lower at the Base Exchange, but off-duty sailors Kevin Jeffrie, Craig Gerlach and Troy Sarro prefer to hang out at Horton Plaza, a whimsically designed, avant-garde shopping mall in downtown San Diego.
Photographer:
Joy Wolf

Camp Pendleton's 128,000 acres make it the largest amphibious Marine base in the U.S. Originally, it was part of an enormous Spanish land grant called Rancho Santa Margarita. In 1975, it served briefly as a major receiving center for Vietnamese refugees.
Photographer:
Jerry Valente

● *Left*

At the Oceanside College of
Beauty, student beauticians
practice on wigged manne-
quins before moving on to tint
and curl clients like Loretta
Callahan.
Photographer:
Jerry Valente

● *Left*

For Stanford coeds Kristin
McKillop and Allison Harapat
the school day begins early.
Like most university resi-
dences, Stern Hall houses
both sexes. On this floor even
the bathrooms are integrated.
Photographer:
Michael Bryant

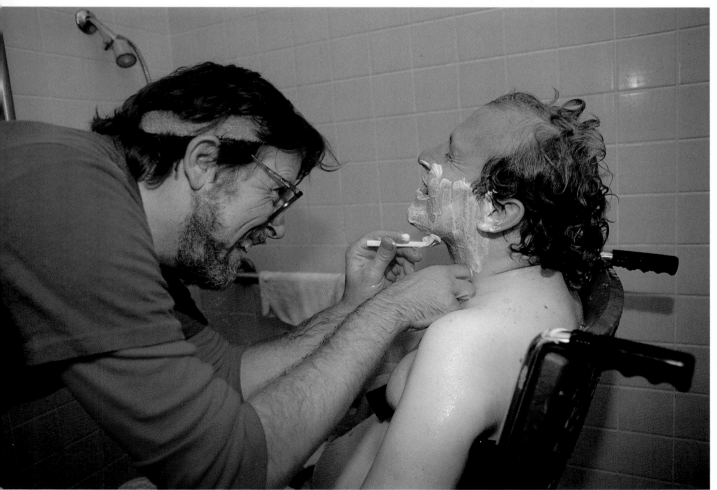

● *Left*

Stockton native Brian Hogan
became a quadriplegic when he
was 17—the result of a bicycle
accident. Getting dressed in
the morning takes him two and
a half hours. But once out the
door, Hogan attends U.C.
Berkeley law school and goes
camping on occasion. "Most
Berkeley students were conde-
scending at first," he remembers. "They assumed I slipped
in on some minority program.
But eventually, a few saw my
test scores and realized I
deserve to be here."
Photographer:
Phillip Quirk

Rick Smolan

● *Left*

Commuting to Redway Elementary school in Garberville.

Photographer:
Bradley Clift

● *Previous page*

On a rainy Friday morning commuters heading across the Golden Gate Bridge have plenty of time to admire the headlands of Marin County. There is always a team of painters at work on the bridge, which is so big that by the time they finish one end, it's time to repaint the other.

Photographer:
Rick Smolan

● *Left*

Boys on the bus: Children attending rural Palos Verdes Elementary School southwest of Tulare in the San Joaquin Valley mug for the camera.
Photographer:
Claus C. Meyer

● *Above*

Eight-year-old Robert Yates is on his way to an acting job in his school play at Lincoln Elementary in the Imperial Valley.
Photographer:
Cristina García Rodero

● *Left*

Stacy Rowell learns her ABCs at the San Juan Capistrano Mission School. Franciscan missions, some more than two centuries old, were the first centers of learning in California.
Photographer:
Don Doll, S.J.

● *Left*

Built in 1895, Petaluma's one-room Union School still teaches children the old-fashioned way. Twenty-five students ranging in age from 6 to 12 all study together in the same room.
Photographer:
Mark S. Chester

● *Left*

Prem Kaur Khalsa supervises 12 children at the Sikh Dharma day-care center in Los Angeles. Besides using the Montessori method, the school also teaches yoga, art and basic health science. There are 4,500 Sikhs in Los Angeles, many of them converts.
Photographer:
Dana Fineman

31

● *Above*

For the children of homeless families staying at Rafael House in San Francisco, school days begin with prayers and the pledge of allegiance.
Photographer:
Paul Chesley

● *Right*

Nearly 3,000 extra people are hired every spring to process the 18,000,000 federal tax returns that flow into the Internal Revenue Service Center in Fresno. "Tingle Tables" (designed by efficiency expert James Tingle) speed the sorting process.
Photographer:
Dan White

● *Right*

Wrap session: First you take a
mud bath at Murrieta Hot
Springs. Then rinse off quick
and dive into a tub full of hot
mineral water. When you
can't take it any longer, get
out. An attendant will come
and wrap you with an ice-cold
sheet. Then lay down and
breathe a mixture of eucalyp-
tus and orange blossoms.
That's aroma therapy. Cost of
the 1-hour-15-minute procedure: $40.
Photographer:
Ed Kashi

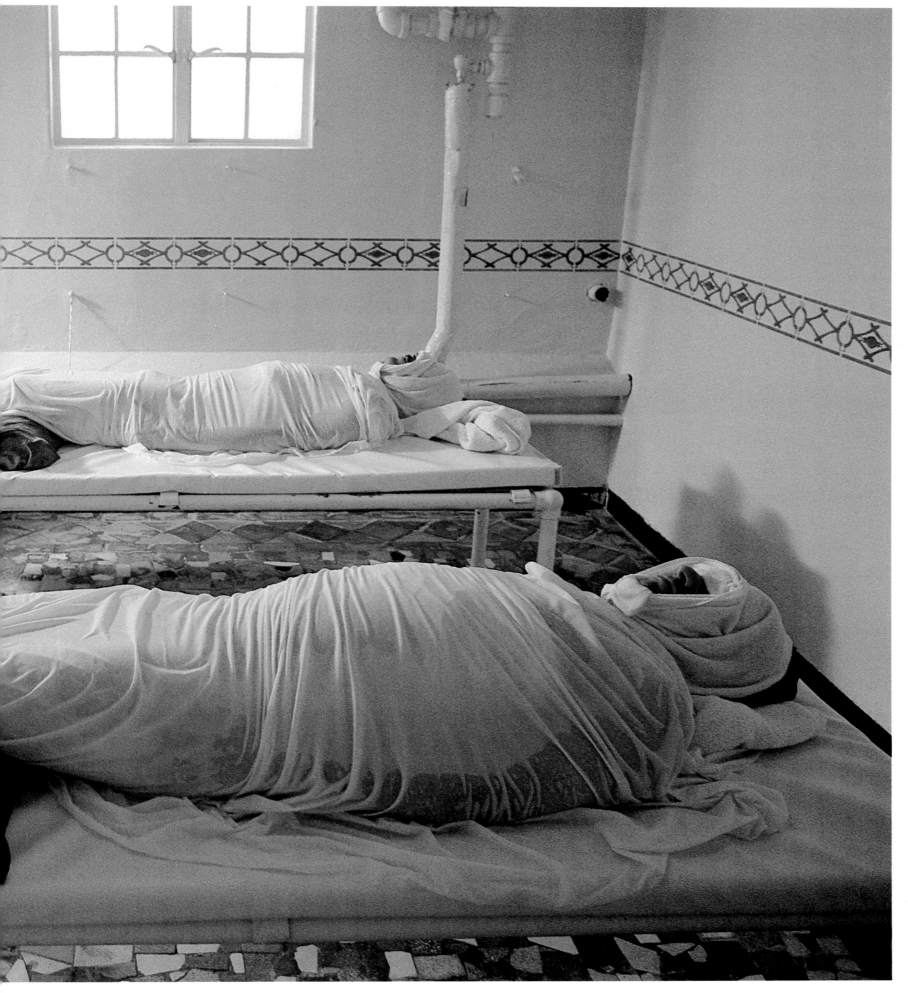

● *Above*

In an advanced-level dance class at Chula Vista High School in San Diego, Laura Fuentes and Susan McComber take a break from rehearsals.
Photographer:
Judy Griesedieck

● *Right*

Ballerinas from across the country come to the Ballet Center for Dance in Marin County. Many of the 600 students board with local families; all hope to become professional dancers. Here Marin's Karianna Jensen, 13, rehearses an interlude from "Unisono," a Dutch ballet being performed in America for the first time.
Photographer:
Jock Sturges

● *Left*

There are no wimps at Gold's Gym, a Venice muscle factory that produces competition weightlifters like Arnold Schwarzenegger and Virginia Brady. On most days Brady can be found at the gym working out with friend and trainer Swale Fenley. Brady holds several weightlifting titles, but doesn't believe they jeopardize her femininity. "My appearance tests people's perceptions of how a woman should look," she says. "When I walk through a crowd, it parts like water."
Photographer:
Sarah Leen

● *Above*

Outside of Gold's Gym, Brady, a mother of two, gives a big hug to her son Timothy when he returns from day care.
Photographer:
Sarah Leen

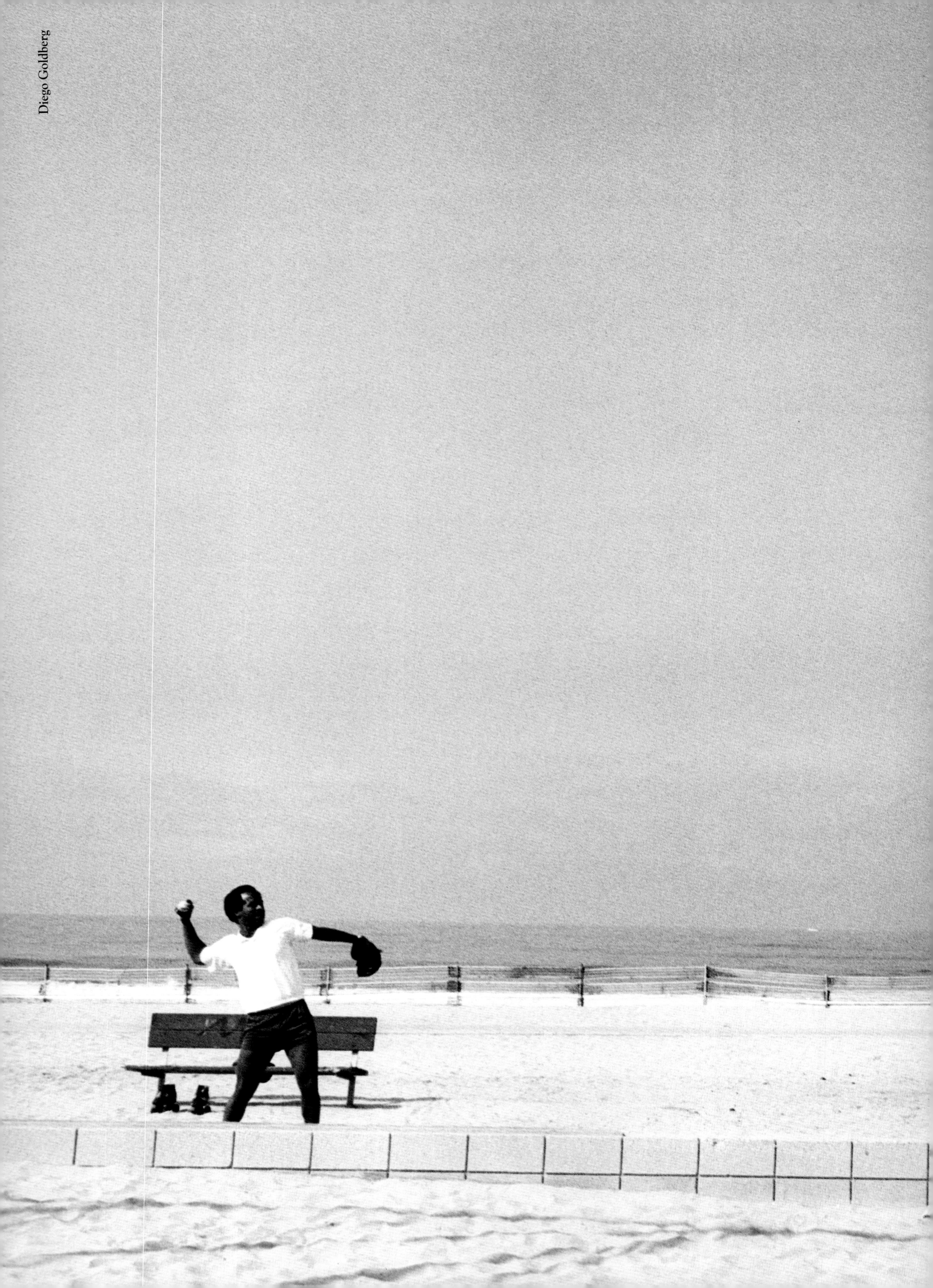

Diego Goldberg

● *Previous page*

Muscle Beach, Venice.
Photographer:
Diego Goldberg

● *Left*

Silhouetted against the
morning sun, free-solo rock
climber John Martin Bachar
heads up "Darth Vader's
Revenge," a rocky escarpment
near Tuolumne Meadows in
Yosemite National Park.
Bachar begins climbing each
spring when the snow melts
and he can find a foothold.
Photographer:
Galen Rowell

● *Above*

Sidewalk surfing may be passé
in some parts of America, but
along Venice Beach there's a
new generation of acrobats.
Photographer:
Diego Goldberg

● *Above*

When editor Bruce B. Brugmann yells, "Copy!" employees at the *San Francisco Bay Guardian* run for cover. California's most outspoken alternative newsweekly zealously maintains its progressive stance. The only conservative thing about the paper is Brugmann's admitted reluctance to use a computer. Seems the "paperless office" just isn't his style.
Photographer:
Michael Downey

● *Right*

On the 20th floor of a new high-rise in San Francisco's Financial District, James Moretti takes a lunch break with the Transamerica building as a backdrop.
Photographer:
Rick Smolan

● *Left*

Louise Burnard is one of the monks living in the Redwoods Monastery, a Cistercian community for women near Garberville in Humboldt county. According to Burnard, the monks consider themselves "spiritual caretakers of the environment."
Photographer:
Bradley Clift

● *Left*

Loggers like Humbolt County's Manuel Freitas still have access to 80,000 acres of "old growth" trees—that is, trees more than 300 years old and 400 feet tall. That worries environmental organizations like Save The Redwoods, which are trying to buy remaining forestland to preserve as parks. Their concern is not unfounded. According to the *Los Angeles Times*, after a company called Pacific Lumber was acquired by a Texas financier in 1986, the pace of logging doubled to pay off high-interest bonds used in the purchase.

Photographer:
Jim Gensheimer

● *Left*

San Jose fireman David
Allshouse.
Photographer:
Doug Menuez

● *Above*

Knight school: Ersatz knights
like Kelly Bailey are a common sight at the Renaissance
Pleasure Faire. During the
week, the fair tries to bring
medieval history alive for San
Fernando Valley school-
children. On weekends,
paying customers can see 900
costumed performers from the
Living History Centre joust
and dance around maypoles.
Photographer:
Bill Greene

● *Left*

Double take: Identical twins Vivian and Marian Brown walk alike and talk alike, and judging from the way one sister will finish the other's sentences, at times they even think alike. The twins, who work as secretaries, are single, but hope to marry someday. They did find romance once at an identical twins convention in Michigan (with another set of identical twins, of course), but marriage plans fizzled when they decided they were matched to the wrong male twin. Vivian and Marian wanted to switch, but the men wouldn't budge.

Photographer:
Ronald Pledge

● *Above*

Born free: These Santa Barbara 3-year-olds seem to have escaped their bonds.
Photographer:
Steve Vidler

Stocking up for the weekend
in Venice.
Photographer:
Diego Goldberg

● *Left*

At a festive birthday party for
two of her friends, Teiko
Iwanaga, 91, performs a
traditional dance she learned
as a child in Japan. The Yu-ai
Kai Center in San Jose
provides a friendly environment for elderly Japanese who
might otherwise remain
isolated at home.
Photographer:
Kim Komenich

● *Above*

Oakland longshoremen Annie
Fuller and her friend Rafael
Aguilar say it takes teamwork
to unload a container ship.
Photographer:
Richard Marshall

● *Left*

On Fridays, a group of Armenians in Fresno congregate at the Asbarez Club. Invariably a spirited debate ensues over whether to play cards or bingo. Pinochle usually wins.
Photographer:
Dan White

● *Above*

Friends: Sister Angela Goldbeck takes a walk with Amber Stewart, age 9, at the Notre Dame Retirement Villa in Saratoga in Santa Clara County. The Notre Dame order emphasizes education of the poor. For more than 50 years, Sister Angela was a grade-school teacher in Los Angeles and the Bay Area.
Photographer:
Kim Komenich

● *Above*

Venice has a large number of retirees, but few are as active as Liz Bevington, 65, who began sailboarding more than a decade ago.
Photographer:
Diego Goldberg

● *Right*

One of the best places to windsurf in San Francisco Bay is north of the St. Francis Yacht Club near the Presidio Army Base, just inside the Golden Gate.
Photographer:
Paul Chesley

● *Left*

Compulsive shoppers like University of San Diego student Mark Wyckoff find that things are cheaper in bulk at the Price Club. A members-only chain of wholesale warehouses based in San Diego, the 24 California Price Clubs attract customers who like to purchase automobile tires along with their toothpaste and regard a seven-gallon drum of tomato paste as an impulse buy. Some club members need a large flat-bed cart to haul the merchandise to their car. Price Clubs are huge, the size of several football fields. If there was a consumer market for cut-rate Boeing 727s, two could easily fit inside one of the stores.
Photographer:
Barry Lewis

● *Left*

Return of the natives: Orange County surfers were really bummed out when former President Richard Nixon proclaimed his San Clemente home the Western White House. They didn't have anything against the man politically—even surfers are Republican in Orange County. But his action allowed the Secret Service to close the Trestles, a beach in front of the house. The Trestles was beyond far-out. It had a radical break and a curl that could only be described as tubular. Today, the Trestles is open again to surfers.
Photographer:
Torin Boyd

● *Left*

Faster than a speeding Angora; more agile than an all-terrain vehicle: Outside of Valley Ford up in Sonoma County, everybody knows Sam the border collie. His mastery of sheep is legendary. Were it not for Sam, his master, Lester Bruhn, would have sold his sheep long ago. "I guess I keep the sheep so Sam can maintain his self-respect."
Photographer:
Jim Richardson

● *Left*

Too young to attend school with her six older siblings, 4-year-old Katrina Westra fills her days with bike-riding, practicing the piano and playing with the neighbor boy. The Westra family is just one of many Dutch families that operate large dairies outside Tulare in the San Joaquin Valley.
Photographer:
Claus C. Meyer

● *Above*

This bull calf probably thinks his branding by Etna rancher Tony Hanna is the low point of the day. Unfortunately, Tony's nephew Greg is waiting in the next pen to perform a procedure called castration.
Photographer:
Joe Rossi

11:30 AM

● *Right*

Outside the Death Valley Pla School in Furnace Creek the temperature can reach 125 degrees in summer. Fortunately, the school has air conditioning, so Melissa and Jason Antonich can stay coo at nap time.
Photographer:
Jonathan Pite

● *Right*

The Sutter Street Head Start Center in San Francisco gives 40 preschool children from low-income families the extra instruction they need to enter the first grade. The instruction is largely academic, but health and nutrition deficiencies also are corrected.
Photographer:
Genaro Molina

At the Prescott Elementary School in Oakland, children don't just skip rope. They "double dutch," a complex maneuver where two or more girls jump two ropes which are simultaneously circling in opposite directions.
Photographer:
Angela Pancrazio

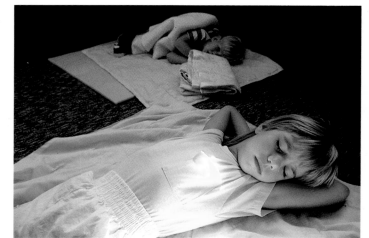

Venice   Sarah Lee

Redway   Bradley Clift

Columbia   Tom Skud

Ojai   Steve Vidler

East Los Angeles   Monica Almeida

Los Angeles   Wally McNamee

● *Previous page*

It took Leonardo da Vinci three years to paint the third wife of a Florentine merchant (a.k.a. Mona Lisa). Lalo Palacios of Gannett Outdoor Advertising in Los Angeles can turn out a reproduction for the Old Spaghetti Factory in 45 days.
Photographer:
Larry C. Price

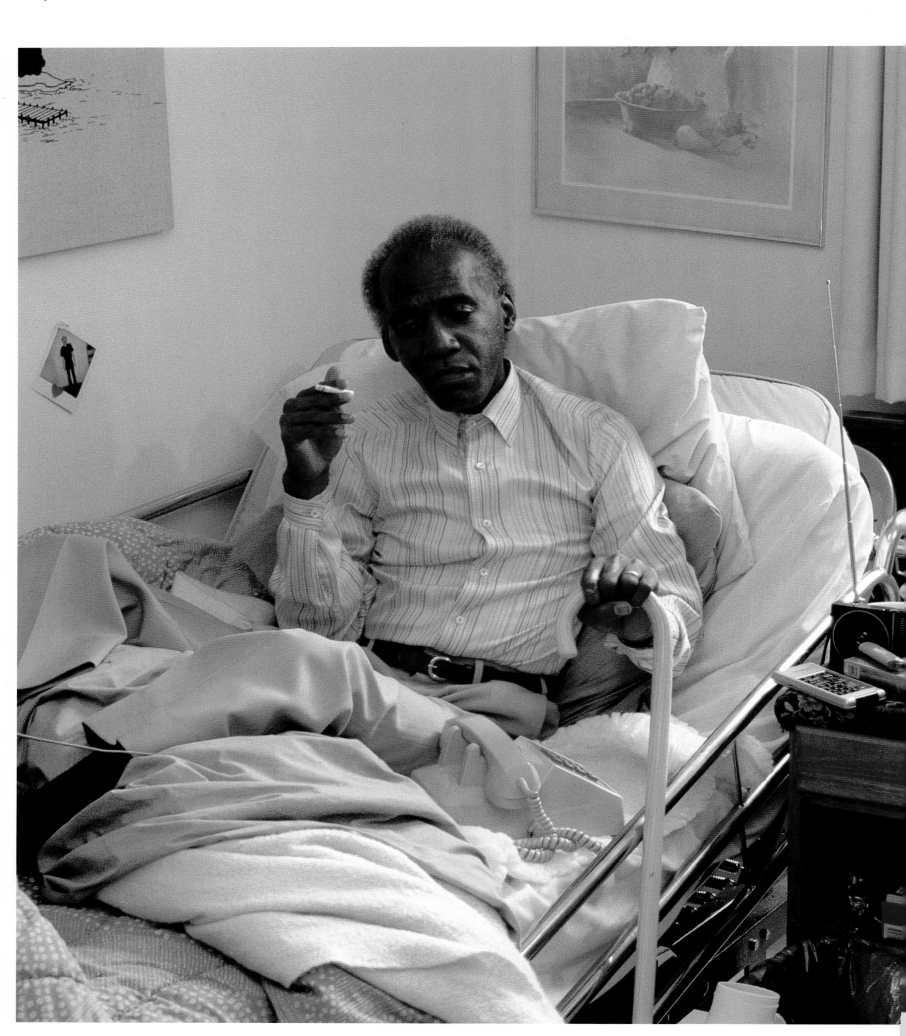

● *Left*

For AIDS patients like Leslie J. Smith at the Coming Home Hospice in San Francisco, life's final months are spent in quiet contemplation.
Photographer:
Alon Reininger

● *Above*

More than 7,500 AIDS-related deaths in California have prompted a new activism in the gay community. On April 29th, demonstrators gathered at a Castro Street plaza named after Harvey Milk, San Francisco's first openly homosexual supervisor, who was assassinated in 1978. The march was organized to protest government policies which hinder Social Security payments to AIDS patients.
Photographer:
Alon Reininger

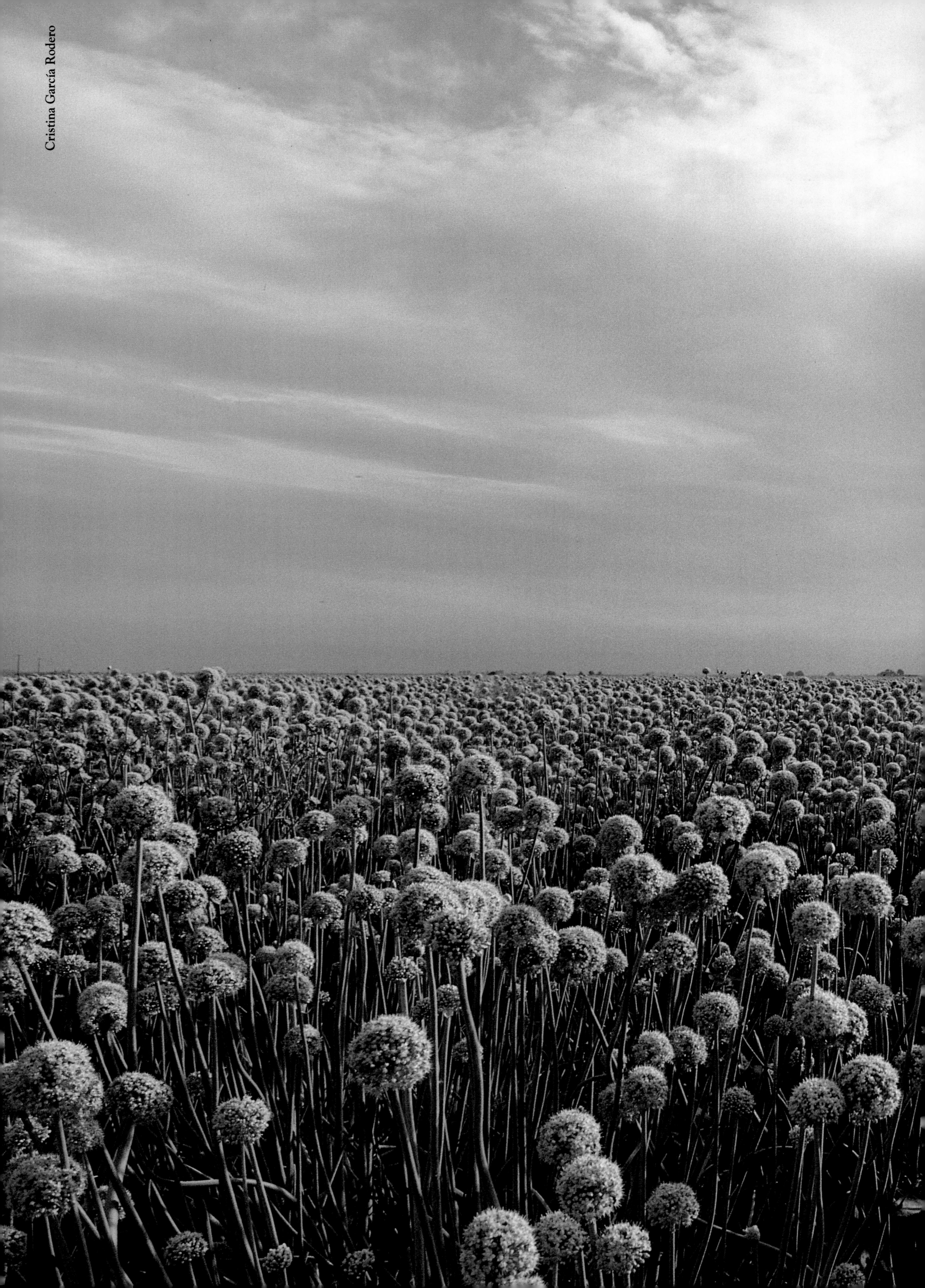

Cristina García Rodero

● *Previous page*

In Southern California, native foliage like Spanish Bayonet belongs to a family of small, shrubby plants called chaparral. Adapted to the region's semi-desert climate, chaparral plants and wildflowers bloom after a steady rain and, ironically, after a fire.
Photographer:
Cristina García Rodero

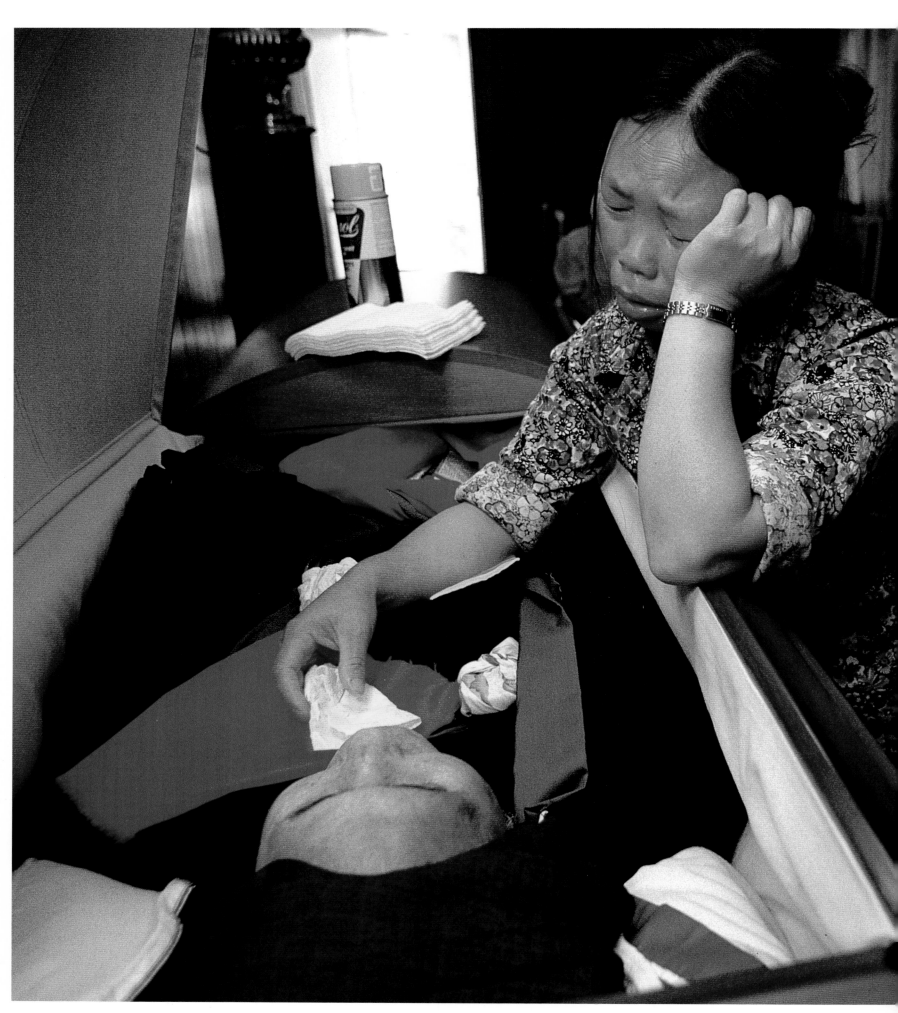

● *Left*

In Fresno, where 20,000 Hmong refugees from Laos have formed a small community, funerals can last up to a week. Shoua Yang has been grieving over the body of her father-in-law, Sia Kao Lee, for several days while another mourner in the background plays a reedy dirge on a hill-tribe instrument.
Photographer:
April Saul

● *Above*

Being a new kid on the block is never easy. But judging by their past academic achievements, Laotian refugee children newly arrived at the Summerset Gardens apartments will adjust rapidly to Fresno.
Photographer:
April Saul

● *Previous page*

Lonely and malnourished with little prospect of employment, Eugene White of Los Angeles made his way to the New Life Institute in Newhall. An all-male tent city with a Christian orientation, the institute provides shelter, emotional support and nourishing meals for 200 residents while they learn a marketable skill such as welding or auto mechanics.
Photographer:
Nick Kelsh

● *Left*

Day in the Life photographer Don Doll is a Jesuit scholar who once taught school on the Rosebud Sioux reservation in South Dakota. When he arrived for his assignment at San Juan Capistrano, he met Father Matthew Krempel, a Franciscan friar from Michigan on a pilgrimage to California. Together they fed the pigeons, then went to pray. Later, Doll followed other Franciscan brothers out into the fields. "Originally, we Jesuits were supposed to come to California," he says, "but after a disagreement with the Pope, pastoral responsibility was given to the Franciscans. They've remained integral to the history of California because of their continuing devotion to the poor and disadvantaged."
Photographer:
Don Doll, S.J.

● *Above*

That's no halo above Mary Ann Wright, but many residents of Oakland's Jefferson Park ghetto consider her a saint. Once a week for the past eight years, "Mother Wright" has been feeding up to 500 homeless and impoverished people with food prepared in her own home the night before. "Loving one another is really what it's all about," she says.
Photographer:
Richard Marshall

Tying the the knot at San Francisco's City Hall on April 29th.
Photographer:
Genaro Molina

Mary-Joy Cabaddu, 22, and Stephen Duffy, 28

Jean Yves Quetalard, 28, and Sandra Hesla, 27

Hansen, 29, and Jan Vaernet, 31, with 5-month-old Rose

Ril Bandy, 40, and Sayoko, 40, with Ril's children from a previous marriage: Allegra, 12, and Ril Jr., age 10

● *Previous page*

Hanging around: According to Manouso Manos, instructor at the Iyengar Yoga Institute of San Francisco, the Rope Headstand "clears the brain and combs the mind." Students Irene English, Carol Cavanaugh, Eve Riebe and Patricia Sullivan—all masters of the intricate toe grip— swear by the exercise, which they say correctly aligns the skeleton. But Manos is sparing with his praise. "Yoga is a continual learning process," he says.
Photographer:
Alon Reininger

● *Above*

Peace activists gather almost every morning outside the Concord Naval Weapons Station in Contra Costa County. Their goal is to stop trains loaded with munitions, which roll out of the armory every Tuesday and Thursday. This vigil for peace was dedicated to one protester whose legs were severed when he failed to move off the tracks in time.
Photographer:
Rick Rickman

● *Right*

On Friday, April 29th, television shows were all reruns because of the Writers Guild of America strike. Television writers earn a minimum of $11,600 for a 30-minute sitcom, $17,000 for an hour. But they and their colleagues in the film industry believe writers' fees and residuals should rise with studio profits. Among other demands, the writers want a greater percentage of foreign sales and a say in how their original manuscripts are produced.
Photographer:
Raphaël Gaillarde

● *Right*

Barbara Hanson, Jennifer Atkins and Lorena Rico are at the Women's Refuge in Redding. "It was incredibly sad," says photographer Yoni Mayeri. "There were women at the refuge who had been battered, disfigured, locked in closets and had watched helplessly while their children were assaulted. Many of these women have no money, no jobs and nowhere to go—and every day they fear for their lives. The shelter offers them a chance to share their pain with other women who understand what they have gone through. The goal is for the women to give each other the self-confidence to stop repeating the pattern which draws them to violent men."
Photographer:
Yoni Mayeri

● *Right*

Friday, April 29th, was another unhappy day for Regina Pinon and her 4-year-old son, Gilbert. Several months before, she and her husband separated. Soon thereafter she discovered she was pregnant. This morning her husband returned, only to serve her with divorce papers.
Photographer:
Maggie Hallahan

● *Previous page*

Battery Point Lighthouse after
a rainstorm, Crescent City.
Photographer:
Steve Krongard

● *Above*

In the far northern county of
Siskiyou, melting snow from
the Marble Mountains feeds a
network of crystalline streams.
Kayakers like Jerry Davidson
test their reflexes amid the
roaring spume of the Salmon
River.
Photographer:
Eric Lars Bakke

● *Right*

The California-Nevada border
runs through the swimming
pool at the Cal-Neva Lodge
on Lake Tahoe. Residents on
the California side insist their
rooms have a better view.
Perhaps—but those staying on
the Nevada side of the pool
can gamble legally and get
married without a blood test.
On either side, the rooms cost
the same.
Photographer:
Jay Dickman

● *Left*

Off the coast of San Diego, Sea World animal-care specialists Nolan Harvey and Brian O'Neil release a yearling elephant seal. Every year Sea World cares for more than 500 injured sea mammals reported by concerned beachcombers. This seal was suffering from malnutrition when it was found beached after a storm.
Photographer:
Bob Couey

● *Left*

California sea otters like the one held by Julie Hymer of the Monterey Bay Aquarium were nearly hunted to extinction at the turn of the century. Rediscovered 50 years ago, there are only about 1,650 of the creatures in the wild today. To prevent their tiny population off Monterey from being wiped out by disease or an oil spill (man and sharks are the otters' only enemies), marine biologists in 1987 began airlifting otters to San Nicolas, an island rich with abalone and crabs 70 miles west of Los Angeles.
Photographer:
Robin Hood

● *Above*

The four California sea otters that live at the Monterey Bay Aquarium are popular with visiting children. They are cute and playful, but their teeth are sharp enough to bite through a lobster claw.
Photographer:
Robin Hood

● *Following page*

Through the looking glass: Barney Garcia from Daly City meets a fellow mammal at the Steinhart Aquarium in San Francisco's Golden Gate Park.
Photographer:
Genaro Molina

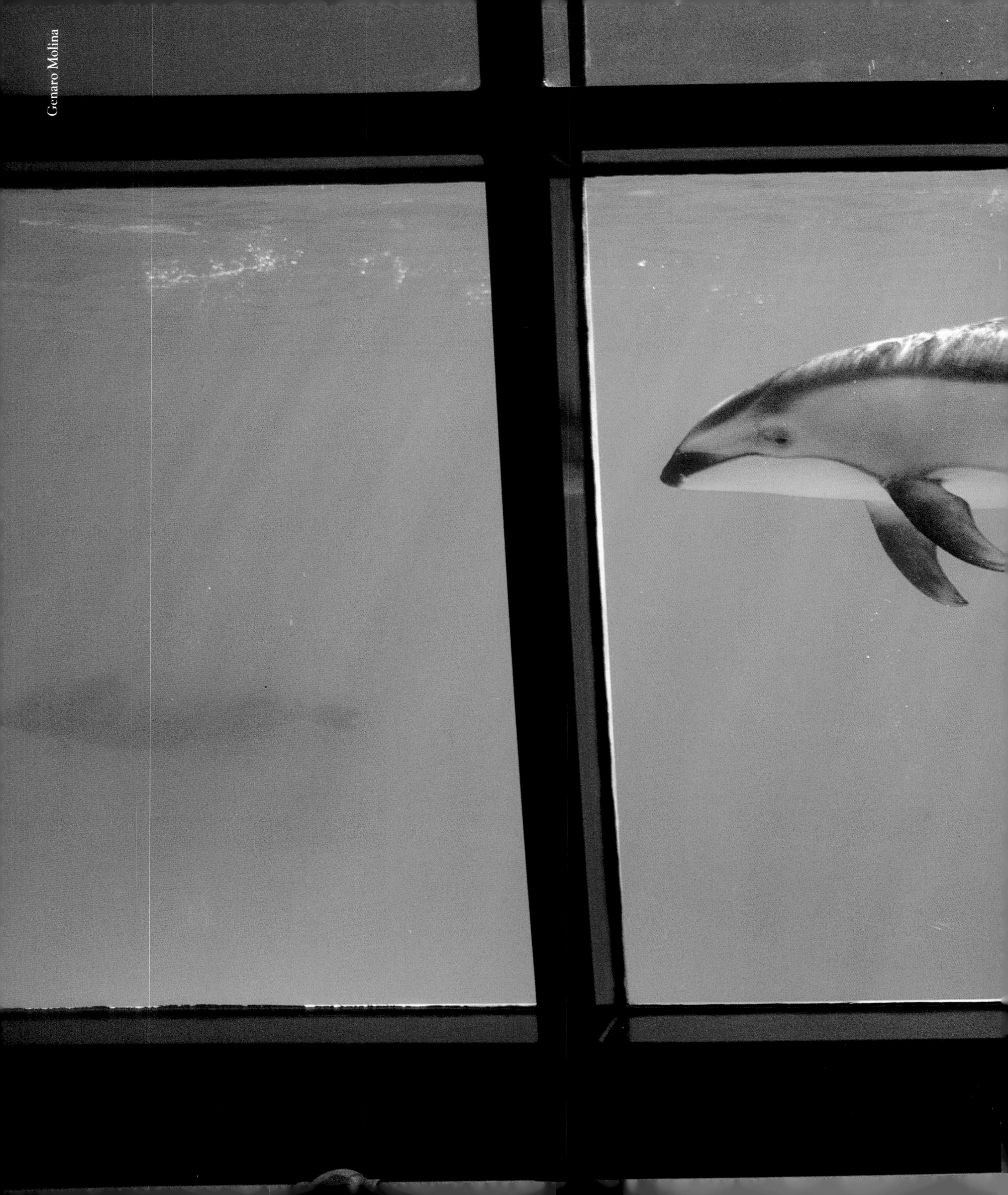

Genaro Molina

● *Left*

Clean-cut conservatives are no longer out of place at Stanford, where '80s students are more career-conscious. With California's presidential primary less than two months away, supporters of Vice President George Bush seem confident of victory.
Photographer:
Michael Bryant

● *Below*

Mark Dimunation, curator of the rare book collection at Stanford University's Green Library, gets so excited when describing the valuable volumes and manuscripts in his care that he can't keep his feet on the ground. "I get teased a great deal about crawling up on the table," he says. "But I really get excited about the knowledge these books will provide students." Among the library's treasures are Freud's original essays on psychoanalysis, original compositions by Beethoven and Mozart, Charles Dickens' *Nicholas Nickelby* in pamphlet form and a Diderot encyclopedia.
Photographer:
Michael Bryant

● *Above, top*

Berkeley University student Brian Hogan, seen on Page 25 beginning his day, is now hard at work in the school library.
Photographer:
Phillip Quirk

● *Above*

On Friday, the subject in Physics 53 is magnetism and electricity. But MarloVan Slate-Teves seems to be thinking more about the approaching weekend in sunny Palo Alto.
Photographer:
Michael Bryant

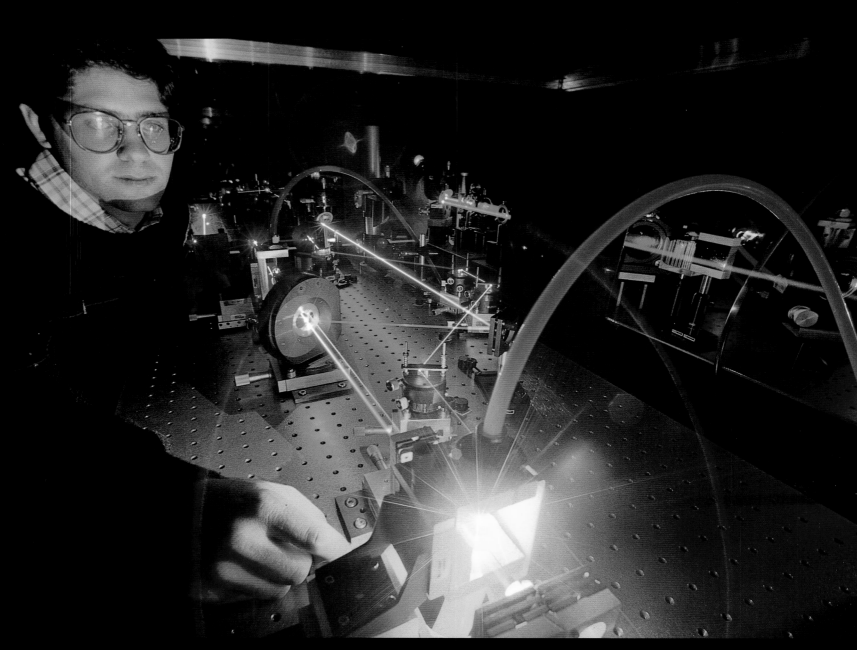

● *Above*

At the California Institute of Technology in Pasadena, pioneering scientific research complements classroom instruction. Here graduate student Marcos Dantus uses laser beams to monitor ultra-fast chemical reactions. In addition to five Nobel Laureates, the Caltech faculty and alumni includes 22 National Medal of Science recipients.
Photographer:
Jim Mendenhall

● *Above*

Though he has lived at the St.
George Hotel in Santa Cruz
for a number of years, Tom

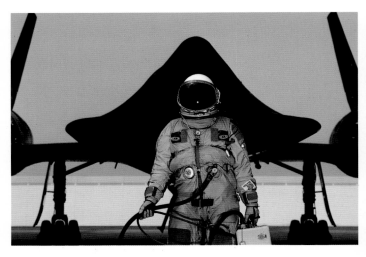

● *Above*

Faster than a speeding bullet:
The SR-71 reconnaissance
aircraft based at Beale Air
Force Base near Marysville
flies at more than three times
the speed of sound at altitudes
in excess of 80,000 feet. At
top speed—which is faster
than the muzzle velocity of a
.30-'06 rifle bullet—it can
photograph more than
100,000 square miles of the
earth's surface in less than an
hour. Although several *Day in
the Life* photographers insist
they have need for such a
plane, the SR-71 is not
currently available for civilian
assignments.
Photographer:
Patrick Tehan

● *Right*

Blowin' in the wind: Experi-
mental aircraft, space capsules
and parts of the NASA space
shuttle all have been tested
inside the Ames Research
Center's wind tunnel at
Moffett Field near San Jose.
Winds up to 350 mph—three
times the force of a hurri-
cane—can be generated by
the large turbines. The 15
people visiting on the morning photographer Roger
Ressmeyer took this picture
are astronaut candidates in
their first year of training.
Photographer:
Roger Ressmeyer

● *Left*

Although calls made from a cellular car phone can cost up to 45 cents a minute (plus long-distance charges), more than 90,000 Los Angeles motorists consider them well worth the money. The densest concentration of California's 20,000,000 registered motor vehicles is in the Los Angeles-Long Beach area.
Photographer:
Douglas Kirkland

● *Below, right*

What a gas: If chemistry student Blake Max seems lost in the ozone, it's because he's breathing laboratory smog similar to that found along the Southern California coast from Pacific Palisades to Corona del Mar. Researchers at Rancho Los Amigos Hospital in Downey hire volunteers like Max to ride a smog-chamber exercycle in order to assess the long-term health consequences of living in America's most polluted metropolis.
Photographer:
Alan Berner

● *Left*

Life in the fast lane: Just west of downtown Los Angeles the Hollywood, Pasadena, Harbor and San Bernardino freeways intersect. Like frontier pioneers, Los Angeles freeway drivers want to know if there's trouble ahead on the trail. Instead of sending out scouts, they listen to traffic reporters like KNX News Radio's Bill Keane who passes on information supplied to him by an airplane, a helicopter and dozens of tipsters who phone in on their cellular telephones. "It's an exciting job—like doing the play-by-play on a sporting event," says Keane.

Every ten minutes for six hours a day Keane tells anxious motorists how to avoid "chrome-crunchers," "bumper-thumpers" and "paint-peelers." Indeed, when Los Angelenos discuss traffic, they speak a language he's largely invented. On rainy days drivers look out for "solo-spin-outs," and "gawkers blocks" caused by motorists ogling smashed cars pushed to the side of the road. They're especially grateful when Keane, a good scout, warns them of ambushes ahead caused by "Smoky handing out greenstamps."
Photographer:
Alan Berner

● *Right*

Louise Curran keeps her cool despite running out of gas in the western San Fernando Valley.
Photographer:
Bill Greene

● *Right*

Have squeegee, will travel: Martgol Beasley and Frank Draughan don't exactly rub elbows with the rich and famous, but they use a lot of elbow grease rubbing their cars. For $200 they will come to your mansion and clean your Rolls inside and out. Female clients sometimes aren't satisfied until their reflections in the hood are clear enough to apply make-up. "There are a lot of car fanatics in LA," Martgol explains with a smile. "If you can't eat off the engine, you didn't call us."
Photographer:
Dana Fineman

● *Right*

With assembly-line precision the 25 employees at the Sunset Car Wash in Los Angeles scrub 150 cars an hour, often while their affluent owners continue to conduct business on cellular telephones. Occasionally, even the fanciest car—in this case a Mercedes 450 SL—fails to start and must be unceremoniously pushed aside.
Photographer:
Douglas Kirkland

● *Left*

Name: Jay Huebert
Age: 29
Occupation: Cowboy for 15 years, now riding 20,000 acres of rangeland near the Nevada border.
Best friend: "My dog, Joe. He does his work and he's my pal."
Frustrations: "Dealing with people who open gates, leave garbage all over, drive through my meadow and don't respect the land."
Photographer:
Galen Rowell

● *Above*

Name: Xavier Becerra
Age: 28
Occupation: Vocalist with the Sex and Cigarettes rock band and a member of the Cathouse bike club.
Hobby: Motorcycle racing at night on the LA freeways. "No cops around and you can make a lot of racket."
Why he rides a bike: "Kinda dangerous. Pick up girls at Hollywood bars. Have fun."
His machine: Despite the T-shirt, Xavier rides a Honda.
Photographer:
Wally McNamee

Migrants passing through Stanislaus County line up early for one of the 91 family units at the Westley Labor Camp. The units cost $80 a month.
Photographer:
Graciela Iturbide

Salvador Estrella is a farm-labor contractor in the San Joaquin Valley. He recruits and supervises migrant workers who are paid $3.35 an hour to work in the fields of the most fertile valley in North America. Here, Estrella's crew is thinning recently planted tomato vines.
Photographer:
Graciela Iturbide

● *Left*

In northern San Diego County near the Mission of San Luis Rey, the same men who do the strawberry picking also wash and package the fruit. "Field packing" is popular with migrant workers, who get a temporary respite from back-breaking harvesting work, and with wholesalers who can move strawberries to supermarkets more rapidly. More than 70 percent of the strawberries grown in America come from California.
Photographer:
Don Doll, S.J.

● *Above*

Father Agustin Ortiz continues the work of the original Franciscan missionaries who moved into California in the late 18th century. A native of Mexico, Ortiz ministers to Indians from Oaxaca who work as migrant laborers outside San Luis Rey.
Photographer:
Don Doll, S.J.

● *Left*

Guillermo Gil, 65, came to California from Mexico more than three decades ago. He found a small house on the outskirts of Seeley, hung the portrait of his father in a position of honor, then went out and found work as an irrigator. As the years passed, Gil says he would occasionally wonder at the end of a long day exactly what he had become. In the spring of 1988 he resolved his dilemma and walked into an Immigration and Naturalization office in El Centro to apply for amnesty and become an American. Gil thinks he made the right decision and believes his father would have approved.
Photographer:
Cristina García Rodero

● *Above*

Every industry has its hierarchy. When it comes to farm labor, the lowest echelon consists of young migrants who trudge into the fields before dawn to pick strawberries. It is back-breaking work. After 11 hours of stoop labor, José Arena, 23, tries to unwind inside the shack he shares with six other men at the Guzman Labor Camp in Soledad.
Photographer:
Nina Barnett

● *Left*

East of Chula Vista, the fence
that forms the U.S.-Mexican
border rapidly disintegrates.
Families walk back and forth
at will. The U.S. Border Patrol
no longer even bothers to fix
the gaps. "Most every family
in Tijuana has a barbecue grill
made out of that fence," says
Border Patrol supervisory
agent Randy Williamson.
Photographer:
Judy Griesedieck

● *Above*

Every night Border Patrol
officers are overwhelmed by a
human wave of illegal immigrants from Mexico. Every 13
seconds patrolmen riding
horses or trail bikes make an
arrest. In 1987, 500,367 illegal
aliens were apprehended, but
thousands more got through.
Illegals who are caught are
held for eight hours, then
returned to Mexico, where
they often try again the
following night.
Photographer:
Judy Griesedieck

Napa and Sonoma coun-
ties, the rolling hills produce
some of the world's finest
pinot noir and chardonnay
grapes. California's wine
industry dates back to the late
18th century when Father
Junipero Serra brought vines
along with Christianity to
California. Until 1848, the
state's vineyards were concen-
trated around 16 of the 21
Franciscan missions in

California. But then thirsty
miners with money to spend
created a market for better
quality wine. In 1861, the
governor of California sent
the superintendent of the San
Francisco mint, Agoston
Haraszthy, on a shopping trip
to Europe. He returned with
100,000 cuttings taken from
300 different grape varieties.
French connoisseurs scoffed,
but Scottish author Robert

Louis Stevenson, a resident of
San Francisco, boldly pre-
dicted, "The smack of California earth shall linger on the
palate of your grandchildren."
Today, California produces 90
percent of North America's
wine, and its grapes are the
state's third most valuable
export commodity.
Photographer:
Pedro Coll

● *Left*

Down in the cellars of the
Rutherford Winery, the
Moreno brothers prepare to
bottle a California cabernet.
Originally from Mexico,
Arturo, Juan and Miguel have
been involved in wine-making
since becoming U.S. citizens
in 1963.
Photographer:
Pedro Coll

● *Left*

At the Demptos Cooperage in
Napa, Will Jamieson, 35, dips,
bends, binds and "toasts"
hand-assembled wine barrels
made from imported french
oak. These stubby, 60-gallon
barrels give a distinctive
character to aging wine.
Photographer:
Pedro Coll

● *Above*

Freewheeling: Tom Wasow, Stanford University's Dean of Undergraduate Studies, bicycles across the quadrangle with flowers for his secretary. Bicycles are the best means of transportation on the university's 8,180-acre campus, which students call "the farm" because it originally served Central Pacific Railroad President Leland Stanford's trotting ponies.
Photographer:
Michael Bryant

● *Right*

With Mother's Day only a week away, Half Moon Bay's Olga Nalle hurriedly prepares 52,000 hydrangeas for shipment throughout the U.S.
Photographer:
Court Mast

● *Following page*

While driving through a scrub-choked desert near Tulelake along the Oregon border, photographer Graeme Outerbridge stumbled onto a fern grotto sacred to the Modoc Indians. "The walls are covered with Indian drawings and all the moss grows upward toward the light. To climb down into this cave and suddenly see water and greenery is truly phenomenal," he says.
Photographer:
Graeme Outerbridge

Tulelake

Graeme Outerbridge

Oakland

Angela Pancrazi

Calabassas

Bill Greer

Camp Pendleton

Jerry Valente

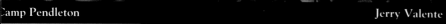

Malibu

Melissa Farlow

San Francisco

David Barry

121

Alan Berner

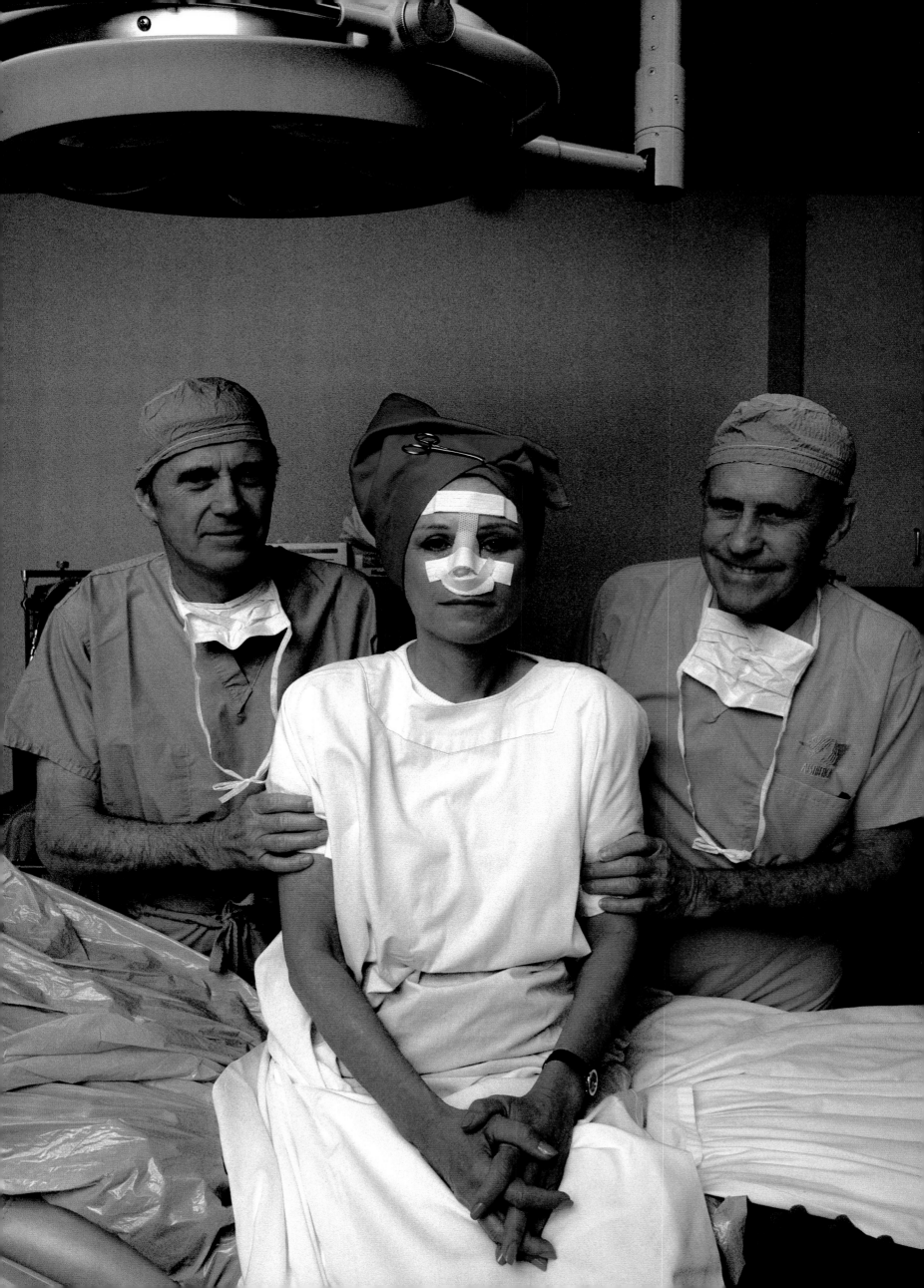

The Victor Clothing Company building in downtown Los Angeles contains numerous bridal shops and is covered with murals. The largest, "The Bride and Groom," painted by Kent Twitchell, depicts a Hispanic wedding.
Photographer:
Alan Berner

Identical twins James and John Williams are Los Angeles plastic surgeons specializing in liposuction (the removal of fatty tissue from the body through a tube) and rhinoplasty (reshaping the nose by removing bone). The Williamses transform photos into three-dimensional computerized images to show potential patients what the results of the surgery will be. They say no matter how exotic the technique, patients invariably remember the experience simply as a "nose job."
Photographer:
Dana Fineman

● *Left*

Los Angeles businessman Roland Silvestri sells his $600 resin-and-polyester mannequins to major department stores in California. Though not anatomically precise, they do aspire to perfection. And what are the measurements of the ideal body? "During the 1950s, my female mannequins were size 12 and had a lot more meat on their bones," he smiles. "Today, stores want a size 6 mannequin that stands exactly 5 feet 10 inches."
Photographer:
Raphaël Gaillarde

● *Left*

When photographer Rick Smolan saw the sign "Have Your Aura Read—$5," he knew he'd found San Francisco's Whole Life Expo, a festival of consciousness-raising where everything from rolfing (shown left) to self-realization was available—for a fee. "All the people were faith-healing, reading auras and buying magic crystals. It was a bizarre bazaar where everyone was trying to sell each other the secrets of the universe."
Photographer:
Rick Smolan

● *Left*

Bee movie: When a script calls for "killer bees," Hollywood gives University of California at Davis entomologist Norman Gary a buzz. A professional insect behaviorist and amateur jazz musician, Gary can create an appliqué of swarming honeybees by painting actors (or in this case himself) with bee sex hormones. *Day in the Life* photographer Bill Ballenberg was a little nervous about this assignment. "The problem," he says, "is that there are always a few asexual bees. Instead of worrying about lighting, my assistant spent most of his time keeping the bees off me."
Photographer:
Bill Ballenberg

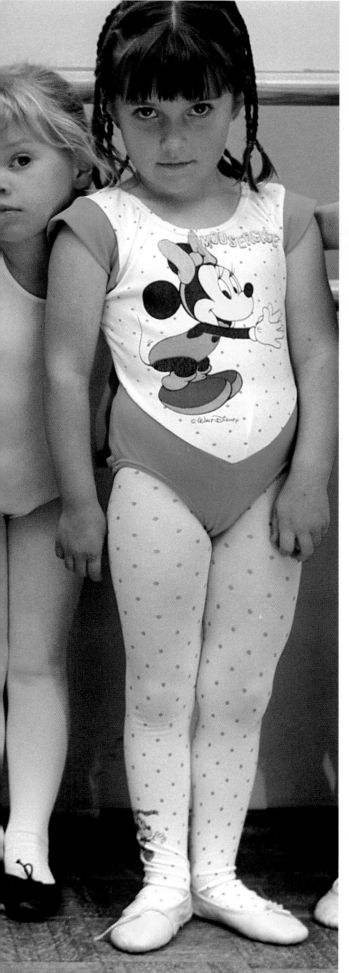

● *Left*

Pretty in pink: Clad in colorful tights, this beginning dance class at Dance Studio 84 takes a break from rehearsing for its spring recital. These 5- and 6-year-olds study jazz, tap and ballet in hopes of developing self-confidence, coordination and poise.
Photographer:
Nick Kelsh

● *Above*

Young skateboarders in Upland in San Bernardino County spend their afternoons at the Pipeline Skate Park. Having mastered the art of "hanging ten" (putting your toes near the board's front edge, causing it to go faster), Danny Montoya, Ricky Bell, Steve Nuñez and Steve Esslinger wait their turn to rocket through a 40-foot-long concrete tube, a maneuver called "shooting the pipe."
Photographer:
Olga Shalygin

Children see the world from a different angle. On Friday, April 29th, Kodak supplied 200 schoolchildren with VR 35mm cameras. In return for working on *A Day in the Life of California*, the children were allowed to keep their cameras. On this page is a selection from the 7,000 photographs shot by this team of young photographers.

Danny Buttke, Age 5   Sebastopol

Amariah Randick, Age 9   Santa Cruz

Christopher Jewell, Age 6   Beale Air Force Base

Tommy James, Age 11   Los Angeles

Jennifer Semana, Age 9   San Francisco

Marisela Lomeli, Age 11   Oakland

Thuy Nguyen, Age 9   San Francisco

Cheng Cha, Age 11   Fresno

Mark Andrews, Age 10   Temecula

Sean MacKenzie, Age 9   Nevada City

Trang Nguyen, Age 10   San Francisco

Nicole Hughes, Age 7   Clearlake

While his wife, Beverly, proudly looks on, Walt Adkins of the San Jose Police Department receives his captain's bars from daughter Charlene. The first black officer in San Jose to be promoted to the rank of captain, Adkins will continue to work as commander of the day-watch patrol division.
Photographer:
Kim Komenich

● *Above*

A church as old and large as
the San Luis Obispo Mission,
completed in 1794, requires a
lot of upkeep. Mary Lou
Limon, one of the many parish

● *Above*

Body shop: Genesis says God created man from a lump of clay. Workers at Silvestri Studio in Los Angeles use resin and polyester.
Photographer:
Raphaël Gaillarde

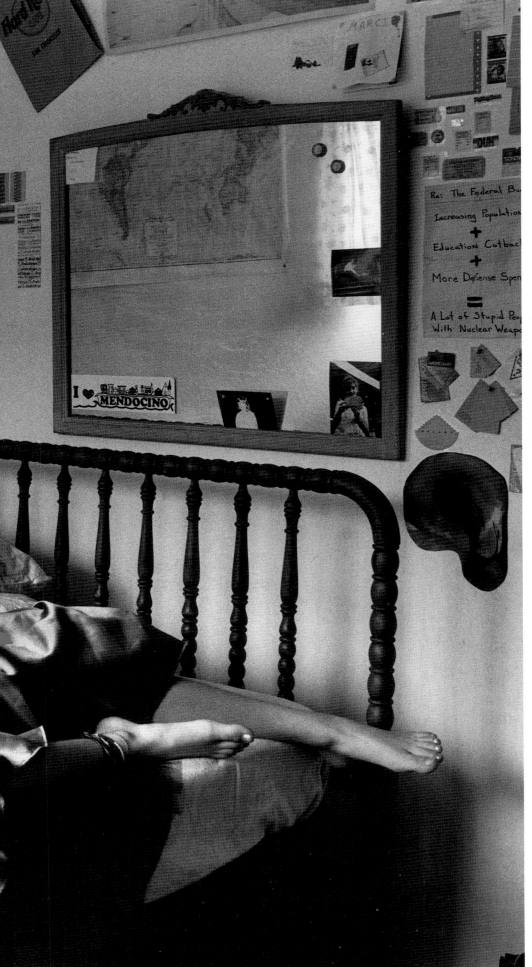

● *Left*

Waiting for Mr. Right:
High school sophomore Marci
Fosse has a problem. With the
big prom only a week away,
the boys in her class still
haven't gotten around to
inviting the girls. On the
afternoon of Friday, April
29th, Marci decided to paint
her toenails and try her prom
dress on while waiting for a
last-minute invitation.
Photographer:
John Loengard

● *Above*

A typical dormroom door at
Stanford University's Stern
Hall.
Photographer:
Michael Bryant

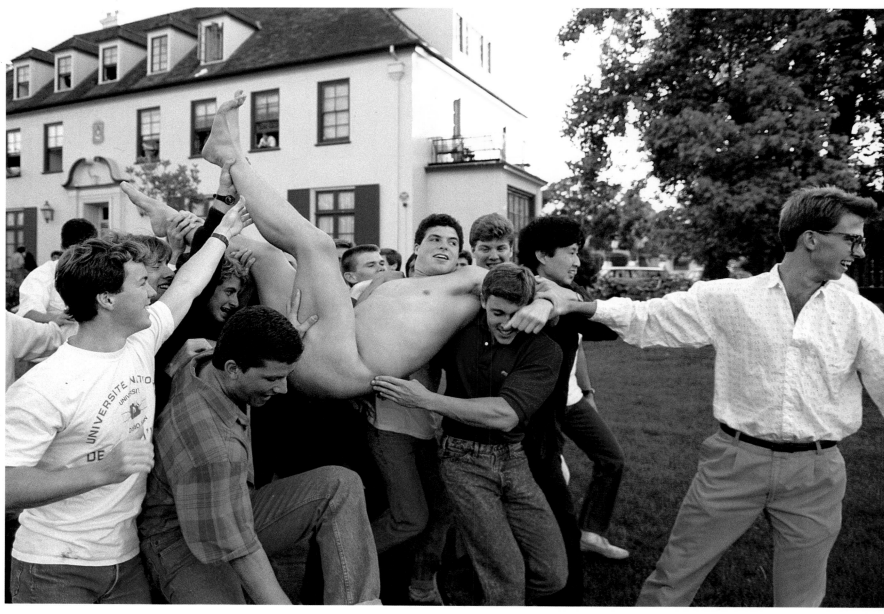

● *Above*

One out of every five undergraduates at Stanford belongs to a fraternal organization. Although hazing has been suppressed, pranks are common, especially during pledge week. Sigma Chi member Robert Miller, here being "stripped and dipped" by the pledges he recruited, will soon be swimming in a fountain in front of the college bookstore.
Photographer:
Michael Bryant

● *Right*

For the past 14 years, the Pegasus Café in Long Beach has been a popular coffee break for truck drivers like Harry Davenport, who hauls newsprint from the San Pedro docks to the *Los Angeles Times*. Harry comes for the cuisine, of course, but the uniforms worn by the Pegasus's waitresses are also part of the coffee shop's attraction.
Photographer:
Nancy Ellison

● *Above*

No bull: Calexico restaurateur Sandra Maria Jesus Bazabal seldom wears the costume she donned as a female matador in Spain for her diners at the Mount Signal Café. But when niece Estrella Vasquez asked to see her aunt's suit of lights, Bazabal complied.
Photographer:
Cristina García Rodero

● *Right*

The ferry home from San Francisco to Larkspur offers the most pleasant commute in California. After a day at the office passengers chat with friends, hack on laptop computers or simply toast each other's health at the bar below deck.
Photographer:
Rick Smolan

Following page

"The Rock": For almost 30 years, Alcatraz Island was America's most intimidating maximum-security prison. Among its more famous prisoners were Al Capone and Robert Stroud, the "Birdman of Alcatraz." After the prison closed in 1963, the island was seized by Indian militants. Today it is part of the Golden Gate National Recreation Area, but some politicians hope it may someday be turned into a casino.
Photographer:
Robert Cameron

● *Right*

Pressing business: A new type of surfer? Militant good-groomers? Your guess is as good as ours. ... But hardly anything surprises anyone anymore on the streets of San Francisco.
Photographer:
Rick Smolan

J eanine Marie Wathen is a detective with the Los Angeles County Sheriff's Department. For the past eight years, she has patrolled the mean streets of Lynwood, a gang-ravaged community (population 86,500) in south-central Los Angeles.

As a teen-ager Wathen wanted to be a veterinarian. But after receiving a bachelor's degree in biological science and a master's in nutrition from the University of California at Davis, she decided to become a police investigator. "I wanted to live an exciting life," she explains. "Now when I wake up each morning I know that the next 12 hours will be completely different from yesterday."

Different, perhaps, but always dangerous. In the '50s classic *Rebel Without A Cause*, teen-age toughs fought with switchblades. Today, Lynwood's gangs prefer Uzis, Mac 10s and other automatic weapons. In truth, Lynwood is a battlefield contested by the Crips, who wear blue, the Bloods, who wear red, and several other gangs. In the past, Wathen has carried a .38-caliber revolver for protection, but now plans to switch to a more powerful 9mm automatic. "Even with a 9mm the bad guys can still outgun me, but at least I'll have a better chance of surviving," she says dispassionately.

In Lynwood the cycle of violence continues without pause. After a crime occurs Wathan identifies, finds and interrogates the suspect. While the investigation continues she consults with district attorneys, continues to gather information and tries to encourage witnesses to testify. She has been offered transfers to other, safer, parts of the county, but chooses to stay in Lynwood to help the law-abiding citizens there. "We have an athletic league, several bicycling events and a community crime-watch program," she says. "There's a lot of interaction between the public and the force."

Photo essay by:
Nicole Bengiveno

● *Left*
Because women's suits are snugly tailored, Jeanine Marie Wathen prefers to carry her .38-caliber Police Special in a purse whenever possible.

● *Above*
"Good cop, bad cop" is a procedure Wathen and her partner, Gary Thompson, use frequently. Here they apply the technique to a suspected mugger accused of snatching a woman's purse the night before.

145

● Below

Along with reserve deputy Linda Brundige, Wathen visits Lugo Elementary School with composite sketches of a child molester who's been approaching young girls. One student recognizes the man. Tomorrow the search will continue.

● Following page

When tensions inside maximum-security penitentiary San Quentin prompt a "lockdown," prisoners monitor the activities of guards and talk "face to face" with inmates in the next cell with tiny mirrors. *Photographer:* **Matthew Naythons, M.D.**

● *Above, top*

Wathen looks through weapons for evidence needed at an upcoming trial. Lynwood detectives confiscate at least two guns a day. By the end of the year their arsenal is the envy of many insurgent armies.

● *Above*

Wathen inspects a prisoner mysteriously wounded in his cell before sending him to the hospital. Lynwood's violence extends inside the jails, but prosecutions are rare since victims know they will be returned to their cells—and perhaps their assailants—after they recover from their wounds.

● *Previous page*

Every April, Little Leaguers like the Yankees in Imperial County take the field.
Photographer:
Cristina García Rodero

● *Below*

Before home games, Los Angeles Dodger rookie pitcher Tim Belcher likes to hang out in the bullpen. Stretching out, he says, is just as important as warming up. Promising players like Belcher enjoy playing in Los Angeles because of public support—more than 3,000,000 fans attend Dodger home games each season—and because games are seldom rained out.
Photographer:
Randy Olson

● *Left*

Maybe you can tell a Dodger without a scorecard, but a trip to Dodger Stadium in Chavez Ravine really isn't complete without buying at least one souvenir from veteran hawker Leroy K. Battle.
Photographer:
Randy Olson

● *Above*

It's always a special day for somebody at Dodger Stadium. Before the Friday night game with St. Louis it was the Indian Guides' turn to be honored.
Photographer:
Randy Olson

● *Left*

Off-duty Marines like Pfc. Christopher Kline from Camp Pendleton can satisfy a yen for cold beer and country music at Carl's Tavern in nearby Vista. *Photographer:* **Jerry Valente**

● *Left*

Built 25 years ago as a country club for Napa Valley vintners, the Meadowood is now a 70-room resort where executives and their families can pay up to $450 a night for a cottage.
Photographer:
Pedro Coll

● *Above*

At the Meadowood in St. Helena the patrician ambiance extends to the manicured croquet green. Here, Robin Lail and Kathleen Belhumeur discuss the progress of their English-style six-wicket match.
Photographer:
Pedro Coll

• *Above*

Its members say the Stanford marching band is unique. Other Pac 10 schools dismiss it as bizarre. But everyone agrees it's entertaining. While other bands move with military precision and stage tributes to Irving Berlin, Stanford's 145 musicians play jazz-rock and skitter unpredictably about the field. In a game against San Diego State, where the halftime theme was "Reasons to Go to San Diego," they spelled out three words: "Zoo ... um ... Zoo." A medley of tunes from *Easy Rider* greeted the release of a report from The President's Commission on Marijuana. But the band's most memorable performance was its "Tribute to Tastelessness," in which its members spelled out "tofu" and "spit," before dropping their pants.
Photographer:
Michael Bryant

• *Right*

No matter whether it's a black-tie performance or just a rehearsal, the San Francisco Symphony Orchestra always takes its music seriously.
Photographer:
Rick Smolan

● *Left*

High atop the Golden Gate Bridge, ironworkers Mitch Chestohin and George Bryden repair handrails on the 36-inch diameter cables that support the world's third-largest suspension bridge. In case you wonder where the toll money goes, it takes 200 employees to maintain the bridge.
Photographer:
Roger Ressmeyer

● *Above*

Outside Livermore, where breezes whipping off the Pacific sweep through a gap in the coastal mountains, ranchers like John Jackson harvest the wind along with their hay. Farmers lease a portion of their land to U.S. Wind Power, which sells the generated electricity to Pacific Gas & Electric. Though corporate investment in solar power has declined, utilities remain optimistic about wind energy. So do farmers like Jackson who now have two sources of income.
Photographer:
Andy Levin

● *Previous page*

A mosaic by Richard Haines decorates the Federal Office Building in Los Angeles' Civic Center. The mural depicts traditional elements of California society. Figures representing family life, labor, science and education stand beside a fruitful "Tree of Life" that shelters citizens pursuing domestic activities.
Photographer:
Wally McNamee

● *Left*

Venice residents pride themselves on their tolerance of eccentrics. But community leaders are less enthusiastic about the hundreds of homeless who moved to the beach in 1987 after an East Los Angeles encampment run by the Salvation Army closed. Stopping occasionally to panhandle, the homeless wander aimlessly during the day, then bed down on the beach at night.
Photographer:
Sarah Leen

● *Above*

Measured by the violence prevailing elsewhere along Skid Row, Crocker Kitchen, an alley just east of downtown Los Angeles, is relatively civilized. The dozen homeless men and women living there hunt for food and firewood during the day. In the evening they return to share a potluck supper, thus giving the alley its name. Recycled shipping crates called "cardboard condominiums" provide shelter.
Photographer:
Randy Olson

Mt. Shasta (population 33,000) tries to limit teen-age graffiti by restricting it to a single location. Spray-can artists are welcome to do their worst at "Graffiti Bridge" out on Old Stage Road.
Photographer:
P. Kevin Morley

When Mono County's Mike Graber wants to soothe sore muscles, he goes to the desert floor of Long Valley where thermal spring water piped into a small crater forms a natural hot tub. "Long Valley is a volcanic caldera where the eastern Sierra runs abruptly into the Great Nevada Basin," says photographer Galen Rowell. "The United States Geological survey posted the whole area on volcano alert four years ago when they found magma under the surface. It's the site of the largest known volcanic eruption in the last million years. I wondered if the guy in the hot tub knew he was sitting on top of a potential volcano."
Photographer:
Galen Rowell

● *Above*

Graffiti in Los Angeles, usually associated with teen-age gangs, has spread beyond impoverished black and Chicano neighborhoods. Gentrified vandals called "taggers" now place their surrealistic monikers through-out the city. Crews of taggers who belong to clubs like "Create to Devastate," "Criminal-Minded Artists" and "Kids Gone Bad" (KGB for short) go on "bombing" missions at night. Their favorite target is the Southern California Rapid Transit District, which will spend $6 million in 1988 (up from $1 million three years before) to remove ink and spray paint from its fleet of 2,500 buses. Some taggers crush their empty paint cans to retrieve the marbles inside, which are then fashioned into bracelets. *Photographer:* **Monica Almeida**

Galen Rowell

● *Left*

Winner's Circle Ranch,
Petaluma.
Photographer:
Jennifer Erwitt

● *Below*

The San Diego Humane
Society invited Karen Payne
and Princess Kitty, a 2-year-
old dancing Siamese, to come
from Miami to perform at its
gala dinner. Princess Kitty is
an established trooper whose
pink tutu and patrician purr
are well known among
fundraisers for East Coast

animal charities. With her
performance just hours away,
the star rehearses on the beach
Photographer:
Barry Lewis

● *Below, right*

Ménage à trois: The southern-most tip of Marin County is a favorite spot for lovers because of its majestic view of San Francisco. With their wedding less than three weeks away, Lothar Heinze and Natasha Schaeffer are reminded by their dog, Outlaw, that he's part of the family, too.
Photographer:
Matthew Naythons, M.D.

● *Above*

Catching some rays on trendy Melrose Avenue in Los Angeles.
Photographer:
Raphaël Gaillarde

● *Right*

They're "Bad": Michael Jackson look-alikes moonwalk down Hollywood Boulevard after checking—"No jobs today, fellas"—with the Central Casting Corporation.
Photographer:
Dilip Mehta

● *Left*

Fresno strolling musicians
Thomas Soma, Antonio Soto
and Francisco Ruiz can always
find an audience for their
mariachi tunes.
Photographer:
Dan White

● *Above*

To earn some spare change,
derelicts on Los Angeles' Skid
Row, and men momentarily
down on their luck like
Rodney Haynes, sell blood to
the Main Street Plasma
Center for $8 a pint. The
AIDS crisis has made the
practice controversial, and
donations are carefully
screened.
Photographer:
Randy Olson

● *Above*

Jenny Brandt, 13, and her cat, Sniffles, in their back yard in North Hollywood.
Photographer:
Melissa Farlow

● *Right*

Raphael Quinemez, Rudy Garcia, Vince Quinemez, Gary Camargo and Woody Sandoval belong to the Northside Watson gang in Watsonville. "We're not nearly as violent as those gangbangers in Los Angeles," says Garcia. "And we're a lot more honorable."
Photographer:
Nina Barnett

● *Following page*

Old-time residents on the Orange County coast weren't too happy when the upscale tract homes of Rancho San Clemente began to cover their golden hills. But complaints abated when the $325,000 dwellings began to sell so quickly that surrounding property values rose.
Photographer:
Don Doll, S.J.

On the Carriza Plain outside Bakersfield in the San Joaquin Valley, ARCO solar mechanic Bob Werner and his dog, Sonny, check some of the 799 "trackers" collecting solar energy for Pacific Gas & Electric. Computer-controlled to follow the path of the sun, the 34-foot-tall panels feed enough current into the PG&E grid to supply the annual electricity needs for 2,000 homes.
Photographer:
George Steinmetz

Made in Japan: Every year an average of 2.5 million Japanese cars are imported into the U.S. Most of those made by Nissan enter through the Port of Los Angeles. Once off the ship, the cars are cleaned, adjusted to meet California's strict auto emissions standards then parked on an 83-acre waterfront lot to await delivery.
Photographer:
Angel Ruiz de Azúa

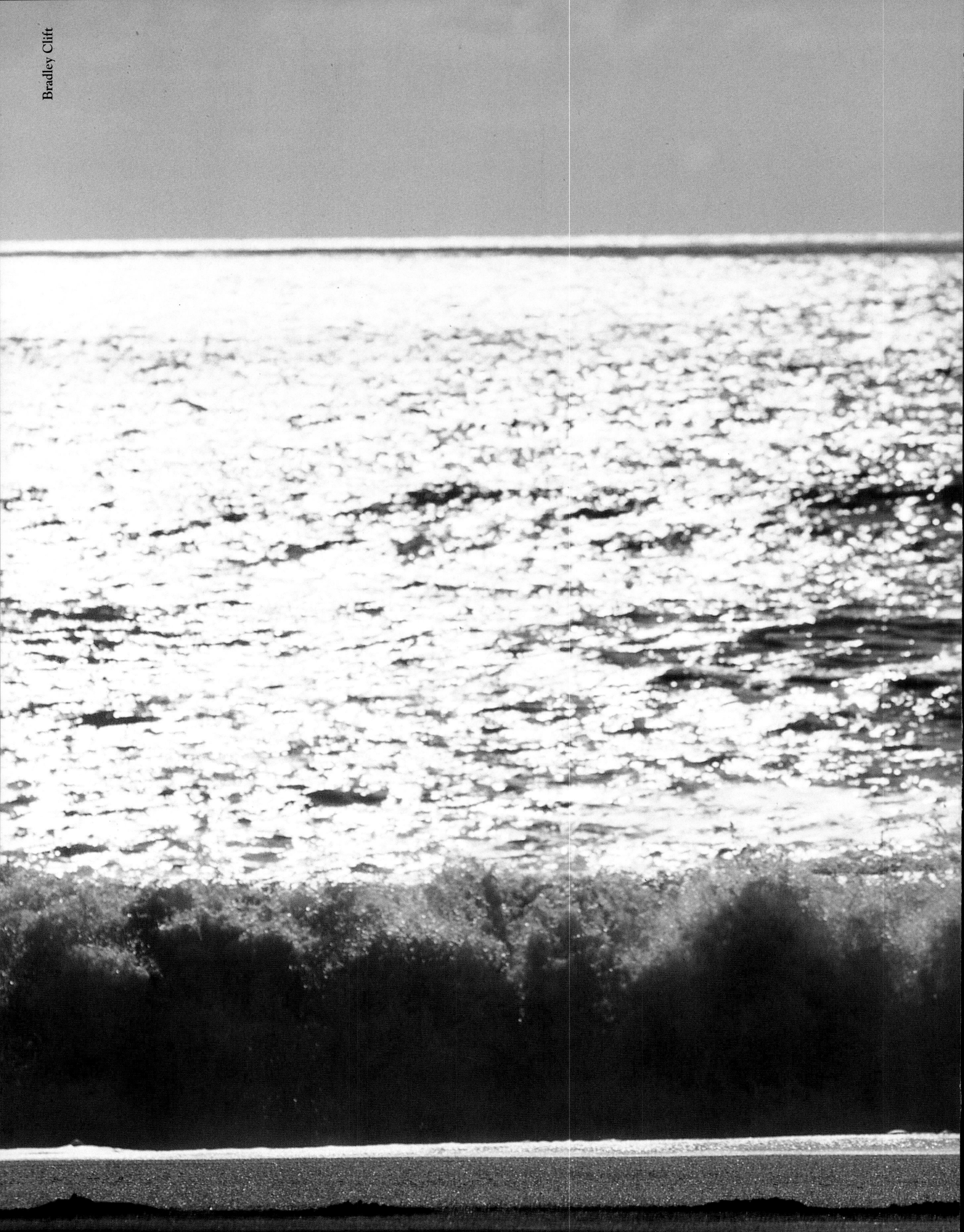

Bradley Clift

● *Previous page*

North of Rockport in Mendocino County, the Pacific Coast Highway veers inward, circumventing a remarkably pristine 76-mile stretch of shoreline called the "Lost Coast." The limited access has impeded commercial development and preserved the wild beauty of a beach happily shared by surfers and horsemen.
Photographer:
Bradley Clift

● *Above*

Latter-day Spanky: Ever since Lana Turner was discovered at the soda fountain in Schwabs drug store, actors with dreams of stardom have flocked to Hollywood where, résumés in hand, they shuttle between casting calls. Drew Joseph Rowe is available if any producer cares to remake the "Our Gang" series.
Photographer:
Dilip Mehta

● *Right*

On the television show "Dallas," oil baron J.R. Ewing is rarely caught with his pants down. But *Day in the Life* photographer Nancy Ellison caught his alter ego, actor Larry Hagman, at home without his chaps. Hagman likes to stay in character, even when going out for dinner near his beach house in Malibu. For the past 10 years, the magic of television has allowed Hagman to live on-screen in Texas and off-screen in the wealthy beach colony which, despite recurring mudslides, floods and fires, is still a haven for Los Angeles celebrities.
Photographer:
Nancy Ellison

● *Left*

It's a dog's world: These wait
patiently for their human on
Santa Catalina Island.
Photographer:
Misha Erwitt

● *Left*

Man's best friend seems to be rethinking the relationship at the Tulare County Fairgrounds.
Photographer:
Claus C. Meyer

● *Above*

Back-seat driver: Traffic delays can be frustrating, even in the small farming communities of the Imperial Valley.
Photographer:
Cristina García Rodero

● *Following page*

The Harbor Freeway links the Port of Los Angeles to Pasadena; Wilshire Boulevard runs from the central business district to the beach in Santa Monica. Just west of downtown they intersect in what home-bound commuters hope will be a blur of traffic.
Photographer:
Nicole Bengiveno

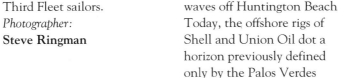

● Previous pages 192-193

Crew-cut palm trees serve as sentinels in Long Beach, California's fifth-largest city and homeport for 12,500 Third Fleet sailors.
Photographer:
Steve Ringman

● Previous pages 194-195

Even before Annette Funicello and Frankie Avalon learned to play *Beach Blanket Bingo*, surfers were catching waves off Huntington Beach. Today, the offshore rigs of Shell and Union Oil dot a horizon previously defined only by the Palos Verdes peninsula and the lyrics of the Beach Boys.
Photographer:
Torin Boyd

● Below and right

Old-time religion: Photographer Richard Marshall of the *St. Paul Pioneer Press Dispatch* spent Friday evening along with 3,000 Pentecostals inside Oakland's Henry J. Kaiser Convention Center attending a "Healing Explosion" led by charismatic evangelists

Charles and Frances Hunter. Pentecostalists believe that evangelists like the Hunters have the power to cast out demons that cause infirmity and disease. "When touched on the forehead by the evangelist, people lapse into rapture and swoon momentarily," the photographer says. "They describe the experience

as 'being slain by the Holy Spirit.' You can't ask for a model release immediately after a person has been slain by the Holy Spirit, but I was willing to wait."
Photographer:
Richard Marshall

● *Left*

Jumping Jack: At Laker play-off games, not all the stars are on the court. Celebrities like Michael Douglas, Dyan Cannon and record producer Lou Adler all have vantage seats near the team's most exuberant fan, actor Jack Nicholson.
Photographer:
Jim Mendenhall

● *Left*

Magic act: Six-foot-9-inch Los Angeles Lakers point-guard Magic Johnson celebrates a play-off victory over the San Antonio Spurs with ice packs and interviews.
Photographer:
Jim Mendenhall

Mr. Mom: When not working as an audiologist for the Long Beach Memorial Hospital Center, John Erratt cooks, cleans and takes care of his 11-month-old daughter, Elizabeth. John's wife, Carolyn, who also works as a speech pathologist for the hospital, does her share around the house as well, but both agree that traditional stereotypes have little meaning when a family needs two incomes.
Photographer:
Gary S. Chapman

Brigid and Anne Rose (first and third from left) have been friends of the Gunnison sisters, Kate and Emelie, for a long time. The Sacramento girls share most everything, and often have slumber parties. But when it comes to revealing dreams in her diary, Anne tells Kate the book will have to remain closed.
Photographer:
Bill Ballenberg

● *Left*

An old Half Moon Bay fishing boat called The Ark serves as a massage studio for Cheryl Fuller, a born-again masseuse who takes a "spiritual and healing" approach to her craft. "I'm a Christian massage therapist concerned with healing the whole person," she says, while kneading the shoulder of Susan Peterson, a fellow masseuse.
Photographer:
Court Mast

● *Above*

After a quick scrub by their mother Gina Cerre, Loren and Lee will be off to bed.
Photographer:
Matthew Naythons, M.D.

● *Below*

The Pontiac Grill is the place to be in Santa Cruz on a Friday night. The 1950s ambiance predates the births of Santa Cruz High School students Kelli Mullen, Stacey Wilhelmsen, Auddrena Mauga and Aimee Nitzberg.
Photographer:
Ricardo De Aratanha

● *Above, top*

New wave: Fraternity pledge Eiji Aono is getting a punk hairstyle from Tri Delt sorority members Stacey Wueste, Corrine Young and Lisa Hellman at a TGIF party at Stanford's Kappa Sigma house. The university's Board of Governors banned sororities (but not fraternities) in 1944, but in 1978, in response to student demand, they were allowed back on campus.
Photographer:
Michael Bryant

● *Above*

And the band plays on: Ernest Vappie, Scott Ortiz and Troy Patterson visit The Stud, one of San Francisco's many gay bars.
Photographer:
Alon Reininger

Yes, we have no Jack Daniels: But Perrier, Evian, Calistoga—even San Francisco tap—all can be had for a modest sum at "The White Room With The Blue Glow," San Francisco's first, and so far only, water bar. Owner Luther Blue serves more than 15 different brands of water while audio tapes of gurgling ocean noise and videotapes of clouds and waterfalls play in the background.
Photographer:
Debra Lex

● *Above*

Tim Ottman sells neon sculptures at Hollywood Neon on Melrose Avenue in Los Angeles.
Photographer:
Raphaël Gaillarde

● *Above*

Girls' night out: To celebrate
Carmen Fregoso's 21st
birthday, her friends hired a
limousine complete with
champagne and accompanied
her to Chippendales, an all-
male striptease review in
Venice.
Photographer:
Sarah Leen

● *Right*

A native of Detroit, Charon
Kivel, 19, dismisses California
as "too plastic." When not
hanging out in Long Beach
with her friends, Skip and
Snot, she adds studs to her
jacket. "You can't buy
anything like this at K mart,"
she says proudly.
Photographer:
Melissa Farlow

● *Following page*

New York photographer
Monica Almeida says she
wasn't scared when she went
on patrol with the L.A.P.D. in
south-central Los Angeles.
"But," she admits, "I sure was
cautious. It felt like a war zone
and at first, I used a telephoto
lens so I could keep my
distance." As the evening
progressed, she grew bolder,
moving in close to photograph
police subduing suspected car
thieves on Slauson Avenue.
But the potential for violence
kept her on edge. "Several
months back, police arrested
three gang members. Now the
gang has a contract out on any
cop they can get."
Photographer:
Monica Almeida

● *Above, top*

At home with her family, Shannon Stewart celebrates her 26th birthday in Redding.
Photographer:
Yoni Mayeri

● *Above*

South of Long Beach, where the Palos Verdes peninsula arcs south into Orange County, lies a series of small beach communities favored by upscale singles. Several years ago, the Beach Cities Community Church decided to create a new ministry especially for these young professionals. It printed notices that read: "New to the area? Looking for an exciting new CHURCH? Desire to meet new friends?" The result is a popular fellowship group that meets every Friday for an evening of song and prayer.
Photographer:
Torin Boyd

● Previous page

In Los Angeles, where the nocturnal glitterati are notoriously fickle, nightclubs blaze to prominence and go nova within a matter of months. On the evening when photographer Wally McNamee passed through town, the favorite spot for Hollywood trendies was the Flaming Colossus, a nightclub that doubles by day as a Knights of Columbus hall.
Photographer:
Wally McNamee

● Below

More than 85 percent of Stanford University's 6,570 undergraduates live in coed residential halls like Yost House, where electrical engineering student Steve Jurvetson burns the midnight monitor. Students with computers don't have to go to the library since a sophisticated network links their terminals to the university's research files. (Students can buy Apple computers, manufactured in nearby Silicon Valley, for half-price.)

For an annual tuition of $11,880, students receive quality instruction from a faculty that includes nine Nobel Laureates, six Pulitzer Prize winners and 11 National Medal of Science recipients. Among the school's more illustrious graduates: three of the nine sitting U.S. Supreme Court justices, former President Herbert Hoover, astronaut Sally Ride and 59 Rhodes Scholars.
Photographer:
Michael Bryant

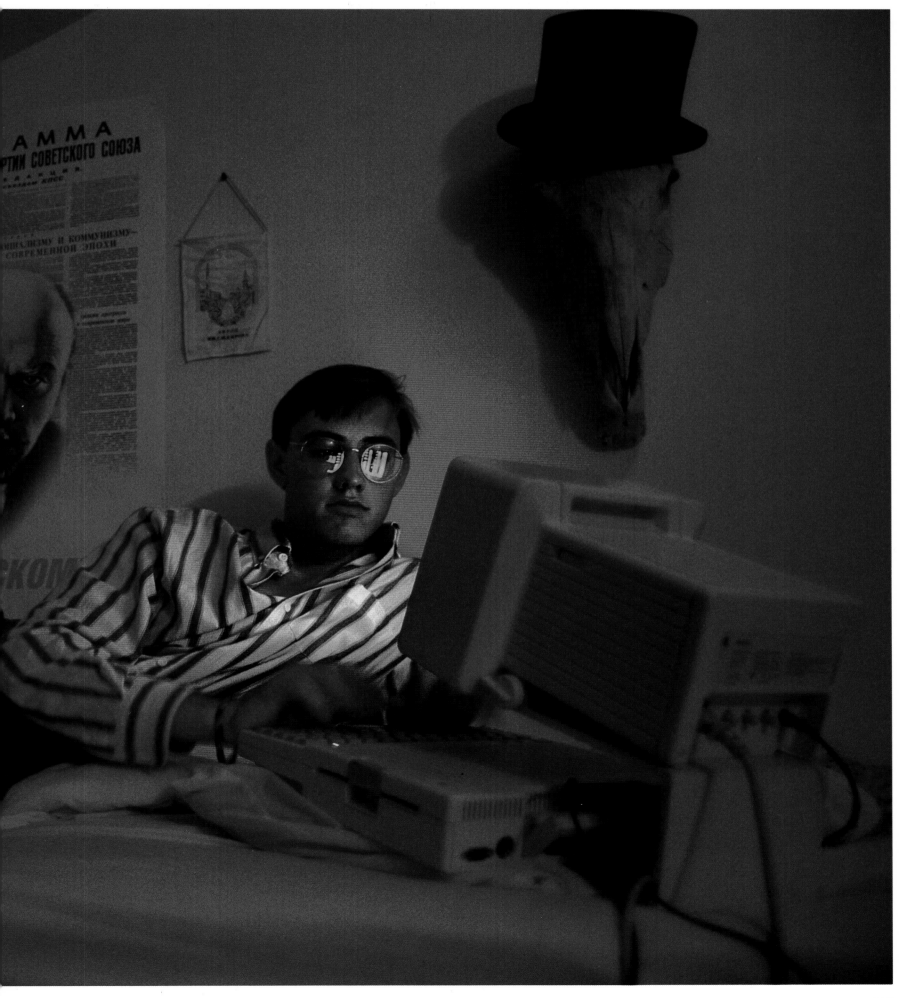

● *Left*

Bohemians break bread with yuppies at Gorky's Restaurant in downtown Los Angeles. The menu is Russian; the walls are covered with paintings by local artists and illumination comes mostly from neon lights like this one resembling the café's namesake, Russian writer Maxim Gorky.

Photographer:
Patrick Downs

● *Above*

After the Chi Omega Spring Formal, the real fun begins at Pasha's Restaurant in San Francisco for U.C. Berkeley seniors Paula Putkey, Chris Kenny and Doug Dupin.

Photographer:
Rick Smolan

● *Above*

Karl Tauber and Janet Mushill arrived at the "Touch of Love" wedding chapel in South Lake Tahoe at 11:48 p.m. At 11:59 p.m. they were declared man and wife. Notary Public and chapel manager Naomi Edmondson took their formal wedding photo; Tauber selected this pose for photographer Jay Dickman.
Photographer:
Jay Dickman

● *Right*

It's still possible to see a movie at Mann's Chinese Theater in Hollywood, but most tourists prefer to compare the size of their feet to those of Marilyn Monroe, Gary Cooper, Sylvester Stallone and the other celebrities who have left a good impression.
Photographer:
Larry C. Price

Matthew Naythons, M.D.

Moonrise over San Francisco.

Doug Menuez

12:00 AM: Lick Observatory, Mount Hamilton, Santa Clara County.

Photographers' Assignment Locations

On April 29, 1988, United Airlines flew the 100 *Day in the Life of California* photographers listed below to San Francisco and to their assigned locations. Our special thanks to United, the only airline able to take on a project of this scope. United Airlines was supported by its marketing partners, United Express-WestAir Airlines, and its interline marketing partners Aerolineas Argentinas, Air France, British Airways, Iberia Airlines of Spain and Mexicana Airlines in this unique venture.

1 Monica Almeida	25 Misha Erwitt	58 Richard Marshall	83 Rick Rickman
2 Eric Lars Bakke	26 Jennifer Erwitt	59 Court Mast	84 Steve Ringman
3 Bill Ballenberg	27 Mark E. Estes	60 Yoni Mayeri	85 Joe Rossi
4 Nina Barnett	28 Melissa Farlow	61 Wally McNamee	86 Galen Rowell
5 David Barry	29 Dana Fineman	62 Dilip Mehta	87 Angel Ruiz de' Azúa
6 Morton Beebe	30 Gerrit Fokkema	63 Jim Mendenhall	88 April Saul
7 Nicole Bengiveno	31 Frank Fournier	64 Doug Menuez	89 Olga Shalygin
8 Alan Berner	32 Michael Paul Franklin	65 Claus C. Meyer	90 Mike Shayegani
9 Torin Boyd	33 Raphaël Gaillarde	66 Genaro Molina	91 Tom Skudra
10 Michael Bryant	34 Sam Garcia	67 P. Kevin Morley	92 Rick Smolan
11 Robert Cameron	35 Cristina García Rodero	68 Robin Moyer	93 George Steinmetz
12 Gary S. Chapman	36 Jim Gensheimer	69 Matthew Naythons, M.D.	94 Jock Sturges
13 Paul Chesley	37 Diego Goldberg	70 Seny Norasingh	95 Hiroshi Suga
14 Mark S. Chester	38 Bill Greene	71 Cheryl Nuss	96 James A. Sugar
15 Bradley Clift	39 Judy Griesedieck	72 Randy Olson	97 Barry Sundermeier
16 Pedro Coll	40 Stan Grossfeld	73 Graeme Outerbridge	98 Patrick Tehan
17 Jack Corn	41 Maggie Hallahan	74 Angela Pancrazio	99 Jerry Valente
18 Bob Couey	42 Bernard Hermann	75 Andrew J. Phelps	100 Steve Vidler
19 Ricardo De Aratanha	43 Robin Hood	76 Jonathan Pite	101 Dan White
20 Jay Dickman	44 Graciela Iturbide	77 Ronald Pledge	102 Joy Wolf
21 Don Doll, S.J.	45 Don Jiskra	78 Larry C. Price	
22 Michael Downey	46 Frank B. Johnston	79 Phillip Quirk	
23 Patrick Downs	47 Ed Kashi	80 Alon Reininger	
24 Nancy Ellison	48 Nick Kelsh	81 Roger Ressmeyer	
	49 Douglas Kirkland	82 Jim Richardson	
	50 Kim Komenich		
	51 Steve Krongard		
	52 Andrew Kruger		
	53 Sarah Leen		
	54 Andy Levin		
	55 Barry Lewis		
	56 Debra Lex		
	57 John Loengard		

Don Jiskra   Skylonda

Morton Beebe   San Francisco

Stan Grossfeld   Cabrillo Beach

Frank B. Johnston   Branscomb

Andrew Kruger   San Francisco

Michael Paul Franklin   Chico

Frank Fournier   Cabazon

• Tulelake/73

• Crescent City/51

• Etna/85
• Forks of Salmon/2   • Mt. Shasta/67

Robin Moyer   Disneyland

Larry C. Price   Beverly Hills

• Eureka/36

• Redding/60

• Garberville/15

• Branscomb/46   • Chico/32

• Fort Bragg/46
• Mendocino/57
• Ukiah/41

Seny Norasingh   San Francisco

• Nevada City/17   • Lake Tahoe/20
• Marysville/98

• Auburn/91

• Sacramento/3
• St. Helena/16
• Santa Rosa/82

• Petaluma/26
• Vallejo/83
• Bolinas/14   • Stockton/27   • Mono Lake/86,96
• Berkeley/71,79
• Marin/6,69,94
• Oakland/58,74,97   • Yosemite/86,95
• San Francisco/5,11,13,22,45,52,56,66,70,77,80,81,90,92
• Livermore/54
• Santa Clara/45   • Modesto/44
• San Mateo/45   • Mammoth Mountain/86
• Palo Alto/10,81
• Half Moon Bay/59
• San Jose/50,64

• Santa Cruz/19

• Salinas/4   • Fresno/88,101

• Monterey/43   • Death Valley/76

• Big Sur/42   • Visalia/65

• Tulare/65

• San Luis Obispo/75

• Bakersfield/93

• Santa Maria/30   • Antelope Valley/34

Sam Garcia   Edwards Air Force Base

• Edwards Air ForceBase/34
• Barstow/48
• Lancaster/34
• Santa Barbara/40,100   • Canyon Country/48
• Newhall/48
• Chatsworth/38 • Pasadena/63
• Burbank/24   • Lake Arrowhead/89
• Hollywood/28,29,33,49,62,78
• Venice/37
• Marina Del Rey/23
• Los Angeles/1,7,8,53,61,68,72,87,96 • Palm Springs/31
• Long Beach/12,84
• Laguna Beach/9
• San Juan Capistrano/21
• San Clemente/9   • Temecula/47
• Camp Pendleton/99
• Santa Catalina Island/25

• Oceanside/99

Jack Corn   Cedar Ridge

Gerrit Fokkema   Santa Maria

• San Diego/18,55,102   • Calexico/35
• San Ysidro/39

Melissa Farlow

During the day I photographed some young punk kids and they invited me to drive down to Long Beach to hang out with them at a party they were having that night. There was this one girl with bright blue hair who was shy. How could you dye your hair blue and then act shy when people gawk at you? But she would hide her face everywhere we went. At the same time she really enjoyed the attention of people passing by. It was that adolescent angst of desperately wanting people to notice you and then hiding when they actually did. The more I was with these kids, the more I liked them. There was something touching about them. We went into a coffee shop late in the evening and they were so embarrassed that someone so normal-looking like me was with them that they told everyone I was their mother!

Claus C. Meyer

I photographed a 4-H fair and I was doing some pictures of these rural kids preparing their animals for the judging—brushing and washing them and so on. The 4-H fair is one of the most important things in their lives because they are all planning to be farmers in the future. The kids are really attached to their animals, and one kid was actually sleeping in the cage with his pig. I photographed one little girl with her rabbit and I asked her whether she would have to sell him after the fair was over. She nodded her head sadly and said, "Yes, and I cry a lot. When we sell them, I cry for two days."

To be or not to be: Bill Ballenberg photographed entomologist Norman Gary at the University of California at Davis.

Wheel life: Photographer Olga Shalygin directs skateboarders in San Bernardino.

A
sk any of the photographers whose images appear on the pages of *A Day in the Life of California* how long it took to produce this book, and chances are they'll say one day. Strictly speaking, of course, they are correct. All of the photographs contained herein were taken during a single 24-hour period. But, like most endeavors where talented people are required to create under pressure, planning was essential. Indeed, the process that brought you *A Day in the Life of California* began many months before the first frame was snapped.

If *A Day in the Life of California* has a genesis, it probably occurred in late 1987 when Collins Publishers moved its permanent headquarters from New York to San Francisco. Neither photographer Rick Smolan nor Editor David Cohen, creators of the *Day in the Life* photography series, moved west with the intention of publishing a book about their new home. The move to California was seen by the pair and their staff as a much-needed change of scene and the perfect reward for having turned out seven *Day in the Life* books in as many years.

Spanish eyes: Publicity Director Patti Richards played hostess to dozens of reporters covering the *Day in the Life of California* shoot, including this team from the Hispanic Broadcasting Company.

After the staff settled into the new offices in San Francisco's North Beach district, Smolan and Cohen debated the possibilities for a sequel to *A Day in the Life of America*, which only a year earlier had become the best-selling photography book in American publishing history. Should they tackle another distant country? After debating whether to do China, Italy, India or France, none of which felt quite right to the staff, they suddenly realized that the answer was surrounding them.

"What really struck all of us about California was the unusual beauty of the cities and the openness among people that seemed so different from New York," Smolan remembers.

In early February, it was decided that California would be the focus of the eighth *Day in the Life* book. A frenzied search for assignment editors commenced immediately. Film industry production coordinator Jain Lemos was lured up from Hollywood. A few days later, photographer Michael Downey and former *Newsweek* staffer Sharon Walters, both living in San Francisco, signed on. The addition of Barry Sundermeier, a former *People* magazine editor, completed the assignment staff.

Before planning could begin, however, the project needed a managing editor—someone who could oversee assignments and serve as liaison with the 100 photographers, someone familiar with and excited about California. It was a critical position that was eventually awarded to San Francisco science photographer Roger Ressmeyer, a veteran of five previous *Day in the Life* books.

Sittin' on the dock of the bay: At Pier 39 in San Francisco, *Day in the Life* staffers Carolyn Cox, Stephanie Sherman, Kate Kelly, Patti Richards and Jenny Barry are joined by 6-month-old Kara Cohen.

The extent of the task confronting Ressmeyer was daunting. California, he soon realized, could easily generate enough assignments to keep 1,000 photographers busy, let alone 100. Joined by Assistant Managing Editor Carolyn Cox, their first task was to somehow select a range of assignments which would capture the diversity and uniqueness of the state while avoiding clichés. "Every year 100 million Americans visit California," Ressmeyer said, "and most of them have cameras draped around their necks." The challenge was to find fresh subject matter and to present familiar sites in ways not photographed before.

As the weeks flashed by, pressure mounted on the team to come up with compelling assignments. Working out of a cluttered office, the editors taped a map of California to the wall, partitioned the state into regions and started placing pins at each possible assignment location. Computer databases and newspaper clip files were tapped for information that, once verified, had to pass other tests. How long would it take to drive to the designated location? Did the subject really lend itself to photography or did it just sound good on paper? Would the photograph surprise readers and give them a new perspective?

With only three weeks remaining before photographers were scheduled to arrive, there were still a few major logistical obstacles. Karen Bakke, a travel agent who had worked on three previous *Day in the Life* projects, was assigned to the massive task of moving 100 photographers and their equipment to San Francisco and then onward to predetermined destinations throughout California. The only problem was that the project still lacked the essentials to get the job done: basics like film, shelter, transportation and money.

Corporate Sponsor Relations Director Cathy Quealy, aided by Production Assistant Monica Baltz, began lining up sponsors. They contacted Ray DeMoulin, head of Eastman Kodak's Professional Photography Division, who offered to donate 6,000 rolls of film—including a few rolls of T-Max P3200, a new black-and-white film capable of being exposed at up to an unbelievable 50,000 ASA. As one photographer later remarked, "This stuff is so sensitive it allows you to shoot in available *darkness*."

United Airlines, sponsor of two previous *Day in the Life* books, came onboard again when its new Chairman, Stephen Wolf, donated tickets to bring all of the photographers to San Francisco from around the world, fly them to their assignments around the state, fly them back to San Francisco to turn in their film and be debriefed, and then fly them back home again.

With the sponsorship by Kodak and United Airlines in place, the project really started to gain momentum. The Hyatt Regency San Francisco volunteered to house all the photographers during their stay in the city. Other hotels and families around the state offered accommodations for the photographers while they were out on assignment. Bank of America and MCI Telecommunications provided additional financing to cover administrative expenses. Hertz offered rental cars. Apple Computer loaned Macintoshes to the project.

Word spread to the media that this year the "Olympics of Photography" were going to be held in California, and Director of Publicity Patti Richards was swamped with calls from around the state. Starting with a front-page item in *USA Today*'s lifestyle section, Richards scheduled hundreds of newspaper, radio and television interviews for the photographers, who were due to show up only a week later.

On Monday, April 25th, photographers from around the world began arriving in the lobby of the Hyatt Regency, and the atrium took on the air of a class reunion, with casually dressed alumni looking as if they had just returned from safari.

"Photojournalists, by the very nature of their work, spend most of their lives in transit," explained Argentine photographer Diego Goldberg, still woozy from his flight up from Buenos Aires. "If it weren't for the magazines I pick up at airport newsstands I'd never know what my friends are doing. These *Day in the Life* projects are the one time each year when many of us get to see, to work and to party together."

Dilip Mehta
Traffic in LA was a real eye-opener. I had just come back from an assignment in Cairo, Egypt, and I thought the traffic there was absolutely insane. But LA traffic made Cairo seem minor. I have been all over the world and never have I seen traffic like this. At one point I missed showing up at one of my locations because I was caught on the freeway for about two hours—and it wasn't even rush hour!

Steve Krongard
My assignment was to photograph a logging operation in Northern California. Before I arrived I was prejudiced against them and the effect they are having on the redwood forests; the way they are destroying part of our nation's heritage. My feelings were confirmed by what I saw from the air—they really are destroying something irreplaceable.
But after spending time with the loggers and talking to them, I realized that most of these guys are in their 20s and for them it's just a job. By the age of 30 they're out of it—they can't keep climbing trees for more than five or six years, and then they end up in a mill and have to work for less money. They weren't evil people, but at the same time I had no doubt that, unrestrained, these guys would cut down every last redwood.
Luckily they're kept in check by the environmental groups. I don't think the logging operations should be shut down entirely, but I think they should be watched very closely.

High-handed: Picture editors cast their votes to choose which shots will make the book.

Chuck Nacke

Rick Smolan

Prints of the city: Picture editors Gary Haynes of the *Philadelphia Inquirer*, George Wedding of the *Sacramento Bee*, freelancer George Olson, Steve Oualline of the *Orange County Register* and Alfonso Gutiérrez of the Spanish agency A.G.E. FotoStock judge black-and-white prints of Los Angeles during the final round of voting.

Eric Lars Bakke

The *Day in the Life of California* picture-editing team: (front row, L to R) Jennifer Erwitt, Steve Oualline, Alfonso Gutiérrez, George Olson, Don Abood, Kate Yuschenkoff, Gary Haynes, Eric Meskauskas, Bill Marr and Dieter Steiner; (back row) Ronald Pledge, Rick Smolan and George Wedding.

Doug Menuez

What appeared to be a disaster at the time may have turned into one of the best pictures of the day. When I arrived at the Lick Observatory just before sunset it was warm and the sky was clear and calm. You could tell that the sunset was going to be just incredible. I planned to wait until the sun actually set, and then to do a shot of the observatory with the sky glowing and the lights of San Jose twinkling down below. To get the right angle I climbed up on top of a 100-year-old water tank that sounded like it was going to collapse at any minute, and I put my camera on a tripod. The sun started to go down, the sky had this beautiful glow and I was about five minutes away from taking the photo, when this 20-mile-an-hour wind came out of nowhere and this amazing storm blew in. Within 20 minutes the temperature had dropped 30 degrees. Being on top of that mountain with the fog swirling below me and the wind blowing faster and faster was exhilarating, but I thought I'd lost any hope of getting a photograph. The fog was so thick I was soaked, and the camera was literally drenched. My hands were frozen. I was cursing the fog and kept waiting for the storm to lift, but it never did. Around 11:30 p.m. I ended up lighting the building with a flashlight, praying there would be enough light. I was pretty delirious by that time.

It was all part of the experience Smolan had envisioned a decade ago when he began promoting the idea of a book—no, actually it would be an event—called *A Day in the Life of Australia*. For Smolan, the goal of the event was not just to produce quality photojournalism, but to create an opportunity for the world's best photographers to renew friendships, compare technique and compete creatively against their most talented peers.

Smolan had gone to Asia at age 26 for a week-long *Time* magazine assignment and ended up staying 11 months. "My only family during that period consisted of other journalists who helped me survive by advising me which border to cross in Pakistan and where to buy refrigerated film in Thailand. All of us traveled constantly, and on those rare occasions when paths crossed, usually in some Bangkok bar, the complaint I heard most often was that our best photographs were often not used. Many of the magazines we worked for were only interested in using our pictures as illustrations."

Today, the *Day in the Life* books have become the most successful photography series in American publishing history. The seven previous *Day in the Life* books (Australia, Hawaii, Canada, Japan, America, the Soviet Union and Spain) have collectively sold close to 2 million copies to date. To put that figure in perspective, most picture books are considered best sellers when they sell 15,000 copies.

It seems incredible now, but in the spring of 1979 when Smolan began searching for financial backing, not one of the 35 publishers he approached believed his concept was commercially viable. It was a gimmicky idea, they said, that would be too expensive to produce. Besides, they smirked, who could imagine 100 photographers—the best in the business—ever showing up at once?

"In retrospect, it was a pretty crazy idea," Smolan now admits. "But we were protected by our incredible ignorance. People either rejected the idea out of hand and laughed at us or fell in love with the audacity of it and offered to help. As more and more creative people got caught up in the insanity we somehow achieved critical mass."

Photographer Galen Rowell directs the group shot (page 224) with help from assistant Lothar Heinze and Cathy Quealy. Carlos Marquez-Sterling records the scene for a one-hour Hispanic television special.

A *Day in the Life* book does not claim to be a complete record of a particular place. Not every city or town can be covered in one short day. Photographers, too, are occasionally disappointed when their work fails to appear. Being a participant in one of photojournalism's most prestigious annual events does not guarantee a photo in the book. When the picture editors make their final selections they are instructed to choose only the best photos, regardless of who shot them. If an assignment does not work out, or the weather is bad or luck turns sour, then that unlucky photographer does not get published. But it is precisely this element of fate that attracts so many world-class photojournalists to work on these projects.

If anything distinguishes the *Day in the Life of California* project from past books, it is probably the number of young photographers—more than 40 in all—invited to participate for the first time. For them the invitation meant admission to the upper echelon of one of journalism's most exclusive fraternities, and, more importantly, exposure in a book that upon publication would immediately become part of the library seen by picture editors around the world. "These *Day in the Life* books serve as great showcases for young talent," explains John Loengard, former picture editor of *Life* magazine. "More than a few careers were launched with a picture published in *A Day in the Life of Australia*."

On Wednesday, April 27th, photographers armed with 60 rolls of Kodak film began leaving San Francisco to spend two days scouting the areas they would be shooting on Friday, April 29th. Before their departure, Editor David Cohen had a final reminder. "When I worked for Contact Press Images in New York we once sent a photographer named Gianfranco Gorgoni to Rome for a story on the Vatican," he said. "About a week later 100 rolls of film arrived back in New York with a one-word caption: 'Pope.' A picture may be worth 1,000 words, but on this project we'd appreciate more detailed information for captions."

Wild thing: The farewell party held at San Francisco's Jukebox Saturday Night was sponsored by the *San Franciso Chronicle* and Kodak. Photographer Graeme Outerbridge of Bermuda and staffer Jennifer Corrigan tripped the light fantastic.

Why are these people smiling? One hundred schoolchildren are about to descend on the Children's Workshop. Seemingly oblivious to the upcoming chaos are Cathy Paver from Pier 39 and *Day in the Life* staffers Monica Baltz, Jennifer Erwitt and Lew Stowbunenko.

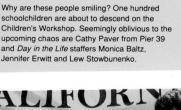

Top dogs: *Time* magazine's local photog, Dr. Matthew Nathons (driving), and his dog, Sashka, give some California "style lessons" to visiting photographers Diego Goldberg of Argentina, Joy Wolf of LA, Dilip Mehta of India, and Robin Moyer of Hong Kong.

For General Manager Jennifer Erwitt, there was nothing to do now but wait. "Even though everything is pretty organized, I know some things can still go wrong," she said. "I'm counting on the photographers to improvise if all doesn't go exactly as planned."

A Day in the Life of California began well before dawn for most photographers. *National Geographic*'s James Sugar was probably the first to greet the new day. Just as the sun peeked over the Inyo Mountains from Nevada, he slipped his tiny plane below the cumulus and arced toward the eastern slope of the Sierra Nevada. He was in pursuit of a magic moment—that flash in time when morning sun turns a mountain from magenta rose to gold.

Click. Whirr. Click. The image blinked through his lens as the camera's motor drive unspooled the film. Ninety seconds were all he would have, perhaps two minutes at the outside. Click. Whirr. The plane roared southward, parallel to the ridge line, held steady by an assistant pilot while Sugar recorded the interplay between mist, shadow and light. Click. Whirr. And then, it ended. The shadows lost their contour; the color began to fade. The plane started to climb, leaving Sugar to wonder if the image on the film would match the beauty he had witnessed.

Dawn found *Time* magazine's Robin Moyer wandering the streets of Disneyland. "The first thing I saw was teams of people steam-cleaning 'Main Street.' They were actually cleaning the cracks and steaming the bubble gum off the streets. By the time they were done the streets were clean enough for the kids to eat off of." Later, in a backstage dressing room, Moyer found himself double-teamed by nervous publicists. Young actors were suiting up, transforming themselves into Goofy and Donald Duck. "Remember, no photos of Mickey without his head," pleaded Matt Blatty, an anxious employee. "The children of America do not want their fantasy destroyed." To the publicists' relief, Moyer agreed to abandon his ambush and went off to shoot Dumbo's Magic Feather.

Boat People: On a Blue and Gold fleet tour of San Francisco Bay, Sales Director Carole Bidnick meets *Day in the Life* photographer Debra Lex.

Out in the western San Fernando Valley town of Chatsworth, Bill Greene of the *Boston Globe* was having problems of a different sort. At 8 a.m. he arrived to photograph a school for stunt people. At 9 a.m. he discovered nearly all of his film was locked in the trunk of his rental car. And the lock was jammed. "I was panic-stricken—afraid that I wouldn't be able to take any more pictures all day," he remembers. "The guys at the school offered to blow open the trunk with some of their explosives. I was almost to the point of agreeing when they finally managed to pry it open."

While Greene's film was being liberated, Philadelphia photographer Nick Kelsh went to the appropriately named Roar Foundation to photograph actress Tippi Hedren's pet tiger. "My idea was to shoot a bird's-eye view of Tippi in bed with the tiger," he remembers. "How was I supposed to know cats don't like things directly over their heads? The cat comes in, looks up at me and does not dig the scene. The cat smells fear." Kelsh quickly suggested that Tippi and the tiger move to another room with a vantage point—in this case a balcony—more remote from the action.

While these events of the morning transpired, Sugar continued to take photos of the aqueducts and pumping stations that bring water from the Owens Valley to Los Angeles. After several take-offs and landings, he discovered—alas, while in the air—that his plane was running out of gas. Spiraling down to the valley floor, Sugar and his assistant pilot landed at Lone Pine Airport, which should have had fuel, but didn't. "Lone Pine's fuel tanks were empty, so we had to hitch into town, buy two five-gallon cans at the local hardware store and fill them at the local gasoline station," says Sugar.

Phuture photographers: At the Pier 39 Children's Workshop sponsored by Kodak, everyone waves to the camera before the lessons begin.

Stan Grossfeld
There's no doubt that California is a special state. It's got everything in it but always with some weird twist. Being an East Coast kid, I'm used to East Coast directness and hostility, but here in California hostility is more subtle—they smile at you first and then they knife you in the back. On the other hand, when I got stuck in the mass of people on the Golden Gate Bridge last year, if they had been New Yorkers they would have panicked and people would have been trampled. Here they are so mellow and well behaved it's disgusting. You know that Woody Allen line: "If he got any more mellow, he'd ripen and rot."

Misha Erwitt
You wouldn't leave two kids unattended in a car in New York or Los Angeles, but on the island of Catalina there is no such thing as crime. Life on this small island is an escape from what the big cities have become. Outside of the tourist season there are less than 100 people on the isthmus side of the island. They work hard taking care of boats and they get paid very little, but what they get back is being able to leave their bicycles outside with no locks. They put up with the tourists in order to have a very relaxed family environment where everybody knows each other the rest of the time. There is a lot of trust there. For someone used to the paranoia of New York City it was really nice to see a place where people liked and trusted each other.

Rick Rickman
I was photographing all these bikers for about an hour in this bar and then they decided to leave. I was packing up my equipment and starting to walk out of the bar when the bartender came over and said I had a bill to settle. I said, "What?" He said the guys in the motorcycle gang had been drinking on my tab! I got stuck to the tune of $125. That was pretty funny. It's not often you get scammed like that.

Rick Smolan

At the same moment Sugar stood beside Highway 395, thumb outstretched, waiting for a ride back to the airport, Stan Grossfeld of the *Boston Globe* was climbing back into bed in his Santa Barbara motel for a late-morning nap. He had just crawled between the sheets when the room began to shake. Says Grossfeld: "The first thing I wondered was, 'How did Smolan find out I was sleeping on the job?' Then I thought, 'Isn't this the state with earthquakes?' I grabbed my clothes and ran out of the hotel. Suddenly, I just didn't feel tired anymore."

Fatigue! By the middle of Friday afternoon, the 300 miles *Seattle Times* photographer Alan Berner had driven since dawn felt more like 3,000. His assignment was to cover Los Angeles traffic and smog and he had seen enough of both to last a lifetime. Realizing he would have little time to eat during the day, he had stocked up on provisions the night before his marathon shoot. Now, the paper bag on the car floor beside him was filled with apple cores, banana peels and wrappers from Tiger's Milk nutrition bars. "On this type of assignment you have to keep going and push yourself really hard. If you stop too long you'll realize how tired you are and then it's all downhill."

Someone well acquainted with exhaustion on April 29th was *National Geographic* photographer Galen Rowell. On that afternoon, Rowell, supported by a single rope, rappelled down a sheer rockface near Tioga Pass in the Yosemite Valley in order to shoot rock climber John Bacher, who climbs the same escarpment without any rope at all.

Another photographer who worked hard to get an unusual vantage point was Patrick Tehan of the *Orange County Register*. To get a picture of a crop-duster pilot above the Sacramento Valley, Tehan wedged himself into a storage bin behind the one-seater cockpit so that he could trigger the remote-control camera he had mounted outside the plane.

For many of the photographers April 29th came to an end all too quickly. The clock struck midnight and the shoot was over. On April 30th the photographers returned to San Francisco with their film, a better-than-average amount of caption material and a new appreciation for California. "Everybody I saw in Southern California was always hustling to get to the next place, or thing or dollar," says Philadelphia freelance photographer Sarah Leen. "But despite the incredible amount of activity, people would always stop and talk politely with me."

At the debriefing session, Production Coordinators Ronald Pledge and Kate Yuschenkoff, along with a dozen other staff members, helped check in thousands of rolls of film. For the photographers the project was over, but for the staff the real work was just beginning. It was a staggering load: 115,000 photographs had been shot during the 24 hours of April 29th, and now those pictures had to be whittled down to a manageable number and turned into a book.

The film came back from processing three days after the photographers departed. Nine leading picture editors, representing many of the world's leading newspapers and magazines, arrived in San Francisco and began pouring over the photographs, voting each one in or out.

After a week of 15-hour days, the pile of photographs had shrunk to the 500 frames referred to as "the final selects." These were handed over to Collins' new Art Director, Jenny Barry, who, sitting down at her Macintosh II, was able to compress what would have normally taken six months of work into six weeks of late nights. Aided by Production Director Stephanie Sherman and Design Assistant Dale Hortsman, *A Day in the Life of California* was finished and ready for the printer less than two months after shoot day.

Before returning home, all of the photographers were interviewed about their experiences and impressions of California. Israeli photographer Alon Reininger seemed to sum up why the *Day in the Life of California* project had captured the imagination of so many people.

"California," says Reininger, "is the most important state in the union—the state of the future. It is the melting-pot tradition of the U.S. come to life. Its relationship with Asia is vastly more important than the East Coast's ties with Europe. Californians influence the taste, cuisine, culture and international awareness of the rest of the country."

A Day in the Life of California is the product of artistic talent and serendipity. Had the photographs been taken on the following or previous day, an entirely different cast of Californians might have emerged. The photographers and editors and hundreds of individuals who helped make this book a reality hope *A Day in the Life of California* will inspire as well as inform. It may take awhile to see if this book becomes a vital part of the history of the state, but everyone who contributed their time and energy hopes that someday, perhaps 40 years from now, when your great-grandchildren ask, "What was California really like back then?" you will be able to dust off this visual time capsule of one spring day back in 1988 and say, "This is the way it was. This was California."

— David DeVoss

Out on a ledge: Assignment Editors Barry Sundermeier, Jain Lemos, Sharon Walters, Michael Downey and Carolyn Cox. That's Managing Editor Roger Ressmeyer in front.

Rick Smolan

Mac attack: Assignment Editor Michael Downey, Sponsorship Director Cathy Quealy and Travel Director Karen Bakke consult the computer to find out when the first wave of photographers is due.

Rick Smolan

Eric Lars Bakke

Group shot: *Day in the Life* staffers (front row, L to R) Karen Bakke, Patti Richards; (2nd row) Cathy Quealy, Rick Smolan, Stephanie Sherman, Monica Baltz, Ronald Pledge; (back row) Larry Kanter, Jennifer Erwitt, Dale Horstman, Jenny Barry, Kate Yuschenkoff.

Photographers' Biographies

Monica Almeida
American/New York, New York
Born in Los Angeles, Almeida began her career at the *Los Angeles Times* where she was on a team of journalists awarded the 1984 Pulitzer Prize for Public Service for coverage of California's Hispanic community. Almeida now works as a staff photographer for the *New York Daily News*.

Eric Lars Bakke   Spain 1987

Eric Lars Bakke
American/Denver, Colorado
A member of the Picture Group Agency, Bakke received an honorable mention for a news picture story at the 1985 Pictures of the Year competition, sponsored by the National Press Photographers Association and held at the University of Missouri School of Journalism. A former chief photographer for the *Denver Post*, Bakke now is a regular contributor to *U.S. News & World Report*, *Business Week*, *USA Today* and *National Geographic* Special Publications.

Bill Ballenberg
American/Virginia Beach, Virginia
A portrait and feature specialist, Ballenberg works for major publications such as *Life*, *National Geographic*, *Sports Illustrated* and *Money*, plus a number of corporate clients. In 1982 and 1983 he was named Virginia Photographer of the Year, and twice (1977, 1983) was honored as Southern Photographer of the Year.

Nina Barnett
American/New York, New York
Barnett is a New York-based freelance photographer whose work often appears in *Fortune*, *Business Week* and *Town & Country*. Barnett also has worked on *Day in the Life* projects in Spain and America.

Morton Beebe
American/San Francisco, California
A corporate, editorial and travel photographer for more than 30 years, this San Francisco native contributes images to *National Geographic*, *Travel & Leisure* and *Time-Life*, and has a long list of major corporate clients. His recent book, *San Francisco*, was a best seller. Beebe has many exhibits and industry awards to his credit.

Nicole Bengiveno
American/New York, New York
Bengiveno is a staff photographer for the *New York Daily News* and is associated with Matrix International. She previously worked for the *San Francisco Examiner*, and was named Bay Area Press Photographer of the Year in 1979. In 1985 she was a finalist for the W. Eugene Smith Award for her documentary work on the AIDS epidemic, and won a first place in feature photography from the New York Associated Press for work in Russia in 1987.

Alan Berner
American/Seattle, Washington
With degrees in philosophy and photojournalism from the University of Missouri, Berner, the 1987 National Press Photographers Association Regional Photographer of the Year, has worked for five newspapers as a photographer, graphics editor and picture editor. He currently is a staff photographer with the *Seattle Times*. While at the *Arizona Daily Star* he received an honorable mention from the Robert F. Kennedy awards for his photos on aging.

Torin Boyd   Moscow 1987

Torin Boyd
American/Tokyo
Boyd began his career as a surfing photographer and then became a photojournalist for *Florida Today*, the *Orlando Sentinel* and UPI. Now based in Tokyo and affiliated with Gamma Press Images, his work is regularly published in *Winds*, *Shukan Asahi* and *Friday*. Boyd's photographs have also appeared in *Newsweek*, *Time* and *L'Express*, and he has served on the editorial staffs of three *Day in the Life* projects.

Michael Bryant
American/Philadelphia, Pennsylvania
A 1980 graduate of the University of Missouri, Bryant worked for the *San Jose Mercury News* from 1980 to 1986, during which time he was named Photographer of the Year in both California and Michigan. Now a staff photographer for the *Philadelphia Inquirer*, Bryant was a 1983 runner-up for the Pictures of the Year Portfolio.

Robert Cameron
American/San Francisco, California
An aerial photographer who began his career with the *Des Moines Register & Tribune* in 1934, Cameron has published three international best sellers: *Above San Francisco* with Herb Caen, *Above Paris* with Pierre Salinger and *Above London* with Alistair Cooke. In 1980 he received the Presidential Award for Photography from President Jimmy Carter for *Above Washington*, and in 1985 he was awarded the Silver Medal of Excellence from the Commonwealth Club of California. For his 1986 one-man show at the Paris Biblioteque Historique, he was awarded La Medaille de Vermeil de la Ville de Paris by Mayor Jacques Chirac. His new book, *Above New York* with George Plimpton and Paul Goldberger, will be released in the fall of 1988.

Gary S. Chapman
American/Louisville, Kentucky
A staff photographer for the *Louisville Courier-Journal's* Sunday magazine and member of The Image Bank, Chapman has freelanced for *National Geographic*, *Time*, *Newsweek*, *Sports Illustrated* and *Forbes*.

Paul Chesley
American/Aspen, Colorado
Chesley is a freelance photographer who has worked with the National Geographic Society since 1975 and travels regularly to Europe and Asia. Solo exhibitions of his work have appeared in museums in London, Tokyo and New York. His work also has appeared in *Fortune*, *Time*, *Esquire*, *GEO* and *Stern*.

Mark S. Chester
American/San Francisco, California
Chester's photographs are part of the permanent collections of the Corcoran Gallery, the Brooklyn Museum and the Lehigh University Museum of Art in Springfield, Mo. A writer with features published by the *Los Angeles Times*, *Boston Globe* and *San Francisco Examiner*, his photos also illustrate *Dateline America* by Charles Kuralt.

Bradley Clift
American/Hartford, Connecticut
Clift has won more than 100 state, local and regional photography awards. In 1986 he won the NPPA Photographer of the Year Award and the World Press Award. Clift presently works for the *Hartford Courant*.

Pedro Coll
Spanish/Palma de Mallorca
Coll is a freelance photographer who works in Spain for A.G.E. FotoStock and for other photo agencies in England, Germany, the Middle East, Australia, the Americas, Asia and the Caribbean. He contributed to the UNESCO book *Patrimonio del Mundo*. A professional photographer since 1975, Coll specializes in geographic photography and has been on assignment in five continents.

Jack Corn
American/Chicago, Illinois
A specialist in documentary photography, Corn is Director of Photography for the *Chicago Tribune*. A contributor to *Time* and the *New York Times*, Corn has been honored by the National Press Photographers Association, and is a recipient of the World Understanding Award.

Ricardo De Aratanha   Burma 1983

Ricardo De Aratanha
Brazilian/Los Angeles, California
A member of The Image Bank and award-winner in the Nikon Photo Contest International, De Aratanha began his career with *Jornal do Brasil*. His work has appeared in *Grand Prix*, *Quatro Rodas*, *Caudia*, *Noticiario da Moda*, *Wisdom* and the *Glendale News Press*.

Jay Dickman
American/Denver, Colorado
A 16-year veteran with the *Dallas Times Herald*, Dickman is a Denver freelancer associated with Matrix International whose work has appeared in *Time*, *Life*, *Fortune*, *Newsweek*, *Bunte*, *Stern*, *GEO*, *National Geographic* and other publications. Recipient of the 1983 Pulitzer Prize, he has been honored with a Bronze Award from Sigma Delta Chi, Society of Professional Journalists, and first-place recognition from the World Press Photo competition. Dickman is a veteran of six *Day in the Life* projects.

Don Doll, S.J.
American/Omaha, Nebraska
Chairman of the Fine and Performing Arts Department at Creighton University, Doll has photographed extensively on the Rosebud Reservation in South Dakota. In 1976 he received special recognition in the World Understanding category of the Pictures of the Year competition. His work has appeared in *USA Today*, the *Seattle Times* and *National Geographic*, plus Collins Publishers' *Christmas in America*.

Michael Downey
American/San Francisco, California
After graduating with a degree in English literature from the University of Oregon, Downey worked as a technical writer in West Germany. In 1987 he attended the Stanford University publishing course. Since then he has worked as a freelance writer/photographer in San Francisco and as an assignment editor for Collins Publishers.

Patrick Downs
American/Los Angeles, California
In his six years with the *Los Angeles Times*, Downs has covered sports and news throughout the U.S. and abroad. He has won top awards from Pictures of the Year, California Press Photographers and the NFL Hall of Fame. His work also has been published in *Sports Illustrated* and National Football League publications.

Nancy Ellison
American/Los Angeles, California
After studying art and exhibiting in museums and galleries in New York, Ellison turned to motion picture photography and celebrity portraiture in 1973. Since then she has worked on such films as *Witness*, *Terms of Endearment*, *Coming Home*, *China Syndrome*, *Farewell to the King* and *Young Guns*. Affiliated with the Onyx Photo Agency, her work appears regularly on the covers of the world's leading magazines.

Misha Erwitt
American/New York, New York
A native New Yorker, Erwitt has been taking pictures since he was 11 and is now on the staff of one of his hometown papers, the *New York Daily News*. He has been published in *American Photographer*, *Esquire*, *People*, *Manhattan Inc.* and *USA Today*. Erwitt has participated in four previous *Day in the Life* projects.

Richard Eskite
American/San Francisco, California
Eskite is best known for his corporate and advertising still-life photography. He has received awards from the San Francisco Art Directors Club, Printing Industries of America, Inc., and consolidated Paper Companies, Inc. His clients include Apple Computer, Del Monte, Ghirardelli Chocolate, Levi Strauss and Raychem Corp.

Mark E. Estes
American/Berkeley, California
A graduate of Houston's High School for the Performing and Visual Arts, Estes holds a B.F.A. in photography from the Kansas City Art Institute. In 1979 he received the Connie Griffith Memorial Photography Award and has since participated in numerous group photography shows.

Melissa Farlow
American/Pittsburgh, Pennsylvania
A staff photographer at the *Pittsburgh Press*, Farlow taught photojournalism at the University of Missouri while working on a master's degree. In 1975, while a photographer for the *Louisville Courier-Journal* and *Louisville Times*, she was on the staff that won a Pulitzer Prize for coverage of desegregation of the public school system. She was the Greater Pittsburgh Photographer of the Year in 1987, and has won honors in the Headliner and National Press Photographers Association Pictures of the Year competitions.

Dana Fineman
American/New York, New York
Fineman studied at the Art Center College of Design in Pasadena. Her work appears in such publications as *New York, People, US, Stern, Time* and *Newsweek*. She is a member of the Sygma photo agency. On May 4, 1986, two days after the shooting of *A Day in the Life of America*, she married photographer Gerd Ludwig. Over 200 of the world's best photojournalists were on hand to cover the event.

Gerrit Fokkema
Australian/Sydney
Fokkema worked for 11 years as a staff photographer for the *Canberra Times* and the *Sydney Morning Herald*. He is now freelancing in the corporate industrial area. His work is on display at the Australian National Gallery, Art Gallery of New South Wales and the Mitchell Library.

Frank Fournier
French/New York, New York
Fournier's work has appeared in a broad array of magazines and journals including *Paris Match, Forbes, Le Figaro, Time* and the *New York Times Magazine*. He won the 1986 World Press Photo Premier Award for Press Photo of the Year and first prize in the spot news category. He is a member of Contact Press Images.

Michael Paul Franklin
American/Escondido, California
Franklin has been a photographer with the *San Diego Union* and *Tribune* for the last four years. Before that he worked at the *Escondido Times Advocate*. He has won many awards for political campaign coverage and food illustration.

Raphaël Gaillarde
French/Paris
Gaillarde is one of the leading news photographers of the Gamma agency. His in-depth coverage of world news events has appeared in many European magazines, including *GEO*.

Sam Garcia
American/New York, New York
Garcia has been a member of the Nikon Professional Services staff more than 12 years. He has helped train America's space shuttle astronauts in the use of 35mm equipment and has photographed several launches. Garcia also has covered most major sporting events, including three Olympics. He has worked on four previous *Day in the Life* projects: Hawaii, Canada, America and Spain.

Cristina García Rodero Spain 1987

Cristina García Rodero
Spanish/Madrid
García Rodero is a freelancer specializing in fine-art photography. Her work has been published in several magazines, including *Lookout* and *El Pías*, and in 1985 she was awarded the Premio Planeta de Fotographía. Previously a drawing teacher, she now teaches photography at the Facultad de Bellas Artes de la Universidad Complutense de Madrid. García Rodero was a photographer on the *Day in the Life of Spain* project.

Jim Gensheimer
American/San Jose, California
A staff photographer with the *San Jose Mercury News* for the past four years, Gensheimer is a 1982 graduate of Western Kentucky University. While at Western, he interned at the *Louisville Courier-Journal* and *National Geographic*, and in 1982 won second place awards in the William Randolph Hearst Foundation Photojournalism Championship and the College Photographer of the Year contest. He has received many honors including Photographer of the Year from the 1984 Atlanta Seminar on Photojournalism.

Diego Goldberg
Argentine/Buenos Aires
After beginning his photographic career in Latin America as a correspondent for *Camera Press*, Goldberg moved to Paris in 1977 as a Sygma staff photographer. In 1980 he moved to New York and in 1985 returned to Argentina. His work has been featured in the world's major magazines, and in 1984 he won a World Press Photo Foundation prize for feature photography.

Bill Greene   Thailand 1987

Bill Greene
American/Boston, Massachusetts
When not covering political turmoil in Haiti, competition for the America's Cup, and news features in Thailand, India and Pakistan, *Boston Globe* photographer Bill Greene collects photography awards. On four occasions he has been named Photographer of the Year by the Boston Press Photographers Association. In 1987 he was honored as National Newspaper Photographer of the Year by the University of Missouri.

Judy Griesedieck
American/San Jose, California
Named Connecticut Photographer of the Year in 1983 while working for the *Hartford Courant*, and California Photographer of the Year in 1986, Griesedieck has been a staff photographer for the *San Jose Mercury News* since 1983. In 1984 she won the Pictures of the Year contest for her "Campaign '84" photo essay on Gary Hart. In 1986 she was runner-up for the Canon Photo Essayist Photo Workshop, and she has won other awards from the Associated Press, National Press Photographers Association, the Pictures of the Year contest and the California Press Photographers Association.

Stan Grossfeld
American/Boston, Massachusetts
An associate editor of the *Boston Globe*, Grossfeld received consecutive Pulitzer Prizes in 1984 and 1985 for his work in Ethiopia, on the U.S.-Mexican border and in Lebanon. His work in Ethiopia also earned two Overseas Press Club awards, one for photographic reporting and the other for human compassion. Since moving to the *Globe* in 1975 from the *Newark Star-Ledger*, he has been named New England Photographer of the Year five times. He is the author of three books, the most recent of which, *The Whisper of Stars*, was released in the fall of 1988.

Maggie Hallahan   San Francisco 1987

Maggie Hallahan
American/San Francisco, California
A native of Northern California, Hallahan has received assignments throughout the world for ten years. She has been a contributor to UPI and the *San Francisco Examiner*. Her work has appeared in magazines such as *Time, Newsweek, Rolling Stone* and *Burda*. She is affiliated with Fovea, Parisian Photo Agency and Network Images in San Francisco.

Bernard Hermann
French/Paris
Hermann started his career working for European newspapers, magazines and the Gamma agency. He later specialized in pictorial books, *Les Editions du Pacifique*, on Tahiti, New Caledonia, New Hebrides, Haiti and Martinique-Guadeloupe. He also has worked on a city series of *Times Editions* on San Francisco, Rio de Janeiro, New York, Paris, New Orleans, Sydney, Honolulu and London.

Robin Hood   Tennessee 1988

Robin Hood
American/Nashville, Tennessee
A graduate of the University of Tennessee at Chattanooga where he studied painting, Hood served as an Army lieutenant in Vietnam. In 1977 he won the Pulitzer Prize for feature photography for his image of a Vietnam veteran. He has published several photographic books and has received awards from Communication Arts, New York Art Directors Club and the Ad Federation Addys for his journalistic approach to advertising photography.

Graciela Iturbide
Mexican/Mexico City
Iturbide uses her camera to capture the poetry of life. She has published two books in Mexico and has exhibited her work in Paris, Zurich and the U.S.

Don Jiskra
American/Chicago, Illinois
Two Jiskra documentaries, *A Touch of Hawaii* and *A Fresh Breeze Across the Pacific*, won awards at the Chicago International Film Festival, the New York Film Festival and the Chicago Industrial Film Festival. Today he photographs scenic destinations for United Airlines.

Frank B. Johnston
American/Washington, D.C.
A former UPI photographer who began his career covering the assassination of John Kennedy and the Vietnam War, Johnston now photographs national news for the *Washington Post*. He co-authored two books, *The Working White House* and *Jonestown Massacre*. Thrice named Photographer of the Year by the White House News Photographers Association, he won an Alicia Patterson fellowship from *Newsday* in 1983 to document social and economic change in America.

Ed Kashi   Nicaragua 1983

Ed Kashi
American/Berkeley, California
When not on assignment for *Time, Newsweek*, the *New York Times Magazine, Fortune* or *Parade*, Kashi freelances for major national and international publications and pursues personal essays of his own. Since 1985 he has been documenting the changes of a small town in Tennessee where General Motors is building its new Saturn plant.

Nick Kelsh
American/Philadelphia, Pennsylvania
Kelsh is a North Dakota native and a graduate of the University of Missouri School of Journalism. He has been the recipient of numerous photography awards for his work, which has appeared in *Time, Life, Newsweek, National Geographic, Forbes, Fortune* and *Business Week* magazines. In 1986 he left a position as staff photographer at the *Philadelphia Inquirer* to co-found Kelsh Marr Studios, a Philadelphia-based company that specializes in the design and photography of annual reports and corporate publications.

Douglas Kirkland
Canadian/Los Angeles, California
Kirkland is one of the world's best-known glamour and personality photographers. Thirty years in the business has included camera work with Marilyn Monroe, Judy Garland, Barbra Streisand, Christie Brinkley and Diane Keaton. He was one of the founding members of Contact Press Images and currently works with the Sygma photo agency.

Kim Komenich
American/San Francisco, California
A two-time National Headliner Award winner, *San Francisco Examiner* photographer Komenich won the Pulitzer Prize in 1987 and the Distinguished Service Award given by Sigma Delta Chi, Society of Professional Journalists. Twice named San Francisco Bay Area Press Photographer of the Year, he was credited with the best news picture story by the National Press Photographers Association in 1983.

Steve Krongard
American/New York, New York
One of America's top advertising and corporate photographers, Krongard's clients include Kodak, Polaroid, IBM, Nikon and Amtrak. He has lectured and taught extensively, and his work has appeared in most major magazines.

Andrew Kruger
Australian/San Francisco, California
A native of Brisbane, Queensland, Kruger, once a political correspondent for the *Sydney Morning Herald*, turned to photography after joining the Australian Associated Press.

Sarah Leen
American/Philadelphia, Pennsylvania
Formerly with the *Philadelphia Inquirer*, where she covered stories in Lebanon and South Africa, Leen now freelances for *National Geographic*. In 1986 she received an honorable mention in the Robert F. Kennedy awards for her story on Alzheimer's disease.

Andy Levin
American/New York, New York
A participant in five *Day in the Life* books, Levin's recent assignments have included coverage of abused children, an orphanage in Guatemala, a ghetto ministry, women in prison, a steamboat wedding on the Mississippi and a quadriplegic basketball-playing Vietnam veteran. He often contributes to *People*, *Parade* and *Signature* magazines.

Barry Lewis
British/London
A freelance photographer for the last 11 years, Lewis has received awards from the Arts Council and *Vogue*, and is a founding member of the Network photo agency. His photographic essays have been published in *GEO*, *The Sunday Times Magazine* (London) and *The Observer*.

Debra Lex
American/Miami, Florida
Currently a contributing photographer for *Yacht* magazine, Lex shoots exciting people doing interesting things for editorial, corporate and commercial clients that include *Boat*, *International*, *Stern*, E.F. Hutton and AT&T. Winner of *Design Annual*'s Award of Excellence, Lex's last book, *Your Future in Space*, featured photographs of NASA's astronaut training program.

John Loengard
American/New York, New York
In 1961 Loengard joined the staff of *Life* magazine becoming, according to *American Photographer*, its "most influential photographer" with essays on the Shakers, Georgia O'Keefe and the vanishing cowboy. When *Life* revived in 1978, he became picture editor. He was the first photo editor of *People*, and in 1982 his essay on photographers, "Shooting Past 80," won first prize in the Pictures of the Year competition. His first book, *Pictures Under Discussion*, was published in 1987.

Richard Marshall   St. Paul 1987

Richard Marshall
American/St. Paul, Minnesota
A three-time regional Photographer of the Year, Marshall began his career as a radio announcer, but found assignments with the *Detroit News* and *Ithaca Journal* more interesting. He currently works for the *St. Paul Pioneer Press Dispatch*. He was chosen Gannett Photographer of the Year in 1985 and has received a variety of state awards.

Court Mast
American/ San Francisco, California
Mast divides his time between surfing and freelance news and sports photography for UPI.

Yoni Mayeri
American/Berkeley, California
A New Yorker who headed west after receiving her B.F.A. in fine art from the City University of New York, Yoni began her career in sales and marketing for such companies as Minolta, Polaroid and Nikon. She now specializes in portraiture and architectural photography.

Wally McNamee
American/Washington, D.C.
During his 30-year career as a photographer, former Marine Wally McNamee has worked for *Newsweek* and *The Washington Post*. He has taken more than 100 *Newsweek* covers and is a four-time winner of the Photographer of the Year award from the White House News Photographers Association.

Dilip Mehta
Canadian/Toronto, Ontario
A member of Contact Press Images, Mehta has covered such diverse subjects as the Bhopal tragedy and political developments in India, Pakistan, the U.S. and Afghanistan. Mehta's pictorial essays have been published in *Time*, *Newsweek*, *GEO*, *Bunte*, the *New York Times*, *Paris Match*, *Figaro*, the *Sunday Times* (London) and other major publications around the world. He has won two World Press Gold Awards and the Overseas Press Club Award.

Jim Mendenhall
American/Santa Ana, California
A staff photographer for the *Orange County Register* when it won a Pulitzer Prize for coverage of the 1984 Olympics, Mendenhall now works for the *Los Angeles Times*. His work has been published in more than 50 magazines worldwide including *National Geographic*, *Forbes* and *Gentlemen's Quarterly*.

Doug Menuez
American/Sausalito, California
Menuez works for *Time*, *Newsweek*, *Life*, *U.S. News & World Report*, *Business Week* and other national publications. A freelance photographer based in Sausalito, he covers the western U.S. on contract for *USA Today*.

Claus C. Meyer
West German/Rio de Janeiro
The winner of many prizes and awards, Meyer was selected in 1985 by *Communication World* as one of the top ten annual report photographers in the world. His color work has been recognized by Kodak and Nikon, and in 1981 he won a Nikon International Grand Prize. He has published several books on Brazil.

Genaro Molina
American/Sacramento, California
Staff photographer for the *Sacramento Bee*, Molina covered Pope John Paul II's 1987 trip to America and the AIDS epidemic in Africa. While attending San Francisco State University in 1984, he was named Bay Area and California College Photographer of the Year. In 1985 he won first place in the Photographer of the Year feature picture competition for his story on a family trying to find housing.

P. Kevin Morley   Richmond 1985

Cheryl Nuss   Sacramento 1987

P. Kevin Morley
American/Richmond, Virginia
University of Missouri graduate Kevin Morley is a staff photographer for the *Richmond Times Dispatch and News Leader*. He is a former coordinator of the Pictures of the Year competition and recently began a program for youth interested in photography.

Robin Moyer
American/Hong Kong
In 1983 *Time* magazine photographer Robin Moyer won the Press Photo of the Year award in the World Press Competition and the Robert Capa Gold Medal Citation from the Overseas Press Club of America for his coverage of the war in Lebanon.

Matthew Naythons, M.D.
American/Sausalito, California
Naythons has spent most of his career alternating between photo coverage of world events and emergency-room duty in San Francisco. In 1979 he founded an emergency medical team to care for Cambodian and Thai refugees. His photographic work appears regularly in major magazines.

THE WALL
Seny Norasingh Washington 1986

Seny Norasingh
American/Raleigh, North Carolina
Born in Laos, Norasingh freelances for *National Geographic*. He previously worked for the *Raleigh News and Observer*, the *Gastonia Gazette* and the *Daily Advance*. He was twice named North Carolina News Photographer of the Year.

Cheryl Nuss
American/San Jose, California
A University of Missouri graduate, Nuss has been a staff photographer for the *San Jose Mercury News* for the past four years. In 1987 she was a Pulitzer finalist for her work on AIDS and was named *Life* magazine's Young Photographer of the Year.

Randy Olson
American/Pittsburgh, Pennsylvania
Olson worked for the *San Jose Mercury News*, *Charleston Gazette*, *Milwaukee Journal* and *West Palm Beach Post* before moving to the *Pittsburgh Press* two years ago. Since then he has twice received the runner-up award for Region 3 Photographer of the Year.

Graeme Outerbridge
Bermudian/Southampton
Named the 1985 Outstanding Person of the Year in Bermuda, Outerbridge is active in both politics and photography. When not working on behalf of the National Liberal Party he submits images to *Vogue*, *Signature* and *The New Yorker*. His first book was *Bermuda Abstracts*. A second on bridges of the world will be published in 1989.

Angela Pancrazio   Walnut Creek 1985

Angela Pancrazio
American/Oakland, California
As a child, Pancrazio, now 31, would clip photos from *Life* magazine to paste on her bedroom wall. Her determination paid off in 1983 when the *Oakland Tribune*, after more than a century of publishing, hired her as its first woman photographer. In 1987 she received an award of excellence in the University of Missouri's Photographer of the Year competition.

Andrew J. Phelps
American/Rochester, New York
A staff photographer with Eastman Kodak's Operational Photographic Group, Phelps excels at fast, on location, available-light photography for major corporate audio-visual presentations. Corporate portrait work and many of his technical photographs appear in national economic and technical publications.

Jonathan Pite
American/New York, New York
When not lecturing on photography or supervising exhibitions of his photos at New York museums, Pite shoots for *Forbes,* the *New York Times* and *Connoisseur.* His corporate clients include AT&T, General Motors and Manufacturers Hanover.

Larry C. Price   Moscow 1987

Larry C. Price
American/Philadelphia, Pennsylvania
Since beginning his career in 1977, University of Texas graduate Price has won two Pulitzer Prizes: in 1981 for his coverage of the Liberian coup, and in 1985 for his photographs of the civil wars in Angola and El Salvador. Currently Director of Photography for the *Philadelphia Inquirer,* his work has been honored by the Overseas Press Club, World Press Photo Awards and the National Press Photographers Association.

Phillip Quirk
Australian/Sydney
Quirk is a founding member of the Sydney-based Wildlife Photo Agency. His work has appeared in most major publications including the *London Sunday Observer,* the *Sydney Times Magazine, National Geographic* and *Time Australia.*

Alon Reininger
Israeli/New York, New York
Contact Press Images co-founder Alon Reininger has traveled the world since 1972 on assignment for magazines like *Time* and *Fortune.* From the presidential campaign of Jimmy Carter and the Sandinista victory in Nicaragua, to China's program of modernization and the ongoing AIDS crisis, Reininger has made a practice of covering breaking news. He has won numerous international awards and plans to conduct photographic workshops in Beijing and Shanghai later this year.

Roger Ressmeyer   Ottawa 1984

Roger Ressmeyer
American/San Francisco, California
One of the country's leading photographers of space technology and science, Starlight Photo Agency founder Roger Ressmeyer also is known for his portraiture. His work has appeared on book covers and record albums by Shirley MacLaine, Grace Slick, Danielle Steel and Judith Krantz. Published in the *New York Times* while an undergraduate at Yale, he later became a regular contributor to *National Geographic, Life* and *Smithsonian.* Today his work is represented by agencies in seven foreign countries.

Jim Richardson
American/Denver, Colorado
Richardson has photographed stories for *National Geographic, Life* and *American Photographer* in addition to publishing two books: *High School USA* in 1979 and *Air Force Academy* in 1986. His documentary photography received special recognition in the World Understanding Award competition in 1975, 1976 and 1977.

Rick Rickman
American/Santa Ana, California
Orange County Register staff photographer Rick Rickman finished 1985 with the Pulitzer Prize for spot news photography and the title of California Press Photographer of the Year. Thrice honored as Iowa Press Photographer of the Year, the New Mexico State University graduate often contributes to major U.S. magazines via his agency, Black Star.

Steve Ringman
American/San Francisco, California
Twice honored as Newspaper Photographer of the Year by the National Press Photographers Association, this *San Francisco Chronicle* staff photographer was California Newspaper Photographer of the Year in 1987 and Bay Area Newspaper Photographer of the Year in 1984, 1986 and 1987.

Joe Rossi
American/St. Paul, Minnesota
A staff photographer at the *St. Paul Pioneer Press Dispatch* since 1983, Rossi has won numerous state awards and participated in Collins Publishers' *Christmas in America* project.

Galen Rowell
American/Albany, California
Rowell frequently photographs and writes about mountains and wild places for *National Geographic, Sports Illustrated* and *Outside* magazines. He has published seven large-format books of his own, the latest being *Mountain Light! In Search of the Dynamic Landscape.*

Angel Ruiz de Azúa
Spanish/Bilbao
Chief photo editor of the Basque newspaper *Deia* since 1980, Ruiz de Azúa has been working for newspapers since age 14. He has worked for the UPI and EFE news agencies, and his photos have appeared in *Paris Match* and *Interviu.* In 1984 he received the Premio Planeta de Fotoperiodismo award.

April Saul   Thailand 1984

April Saul
American/Philadelphia, Pennsylvania
A *Philadelphia Inquirer* staff photographer since 1981, Saul was a Pulitzer finalist for feature photography in 1987. Twice named Pennsylvania Photographer of the Year, she won the Robert F. Kennedy Journalism Award in 1983, and in 1985 received special recognition in the Canon Photo Essayist Award.

Olga Shalygin
American/Redwood City, California
Once a registered nurse, freelancer Shalygin took her first photojournalism course in 1981. Since then she has worked for the *Long Beach Press-Telegram,* the *Hartford Courant,* the *Orange County Register* and the *Los Angeles Daily News.*

Mike Shayegani
Iranian/Los Angeles, California
Shayegani moved to the U.S. from Iran in 1969, and at the age of 14 borrowed his father's Rolleiflex and began to pursue his interest in photography. Once an assistant to glamour photographer Douglas Kirkland, he is now starting a commercial photography business.

Tom Skudra
Canadian/Toronto
Since 1967, Skudra has worked for a variety of clients in Canada and abroad, including the Canadian government, *MacLean's, Equinox, The Globe and Mail* and Labatt's Breweries. He is a three-time winner of the National Magazine Award for photojournalism.

Rick Smolan   Moscow 1987

Rick Smolan
American/San Francisco, California
Former *Time* and *National Geographic* photographer Smolan created the *Day in the Life* series and directed *A Day in the Life of California.* Since 1981 he has organized eight major photographic books: *A Day in the Life of Australia* (1981), *A Day in the Life of Hawaii* (1983), *A Day in the Life of Canada* (1984), *A Day in the Life of Japan* (1985), *A Day in the Life of America* (1986), *A Day in the Life of the Soviet Union* (1987) and *A Day in the Life of Spain* (1988).

George Steinmetz
American/San Francisco, California
Before graduating from Stanford University with a degree in geophysics, Steinmetz dropped out for two and a half years to hitchhike through more than 20 African countries. His work currently appears in *Fortune, Life, National Geographic* and the *New York Times Magazine.*

Hiroshi Suga
Japanese/Tokyo
Winner of the 1987 Ken Domon Award, Suga's photographs have appeared in many international publications, six books and numerous one-man exhibitions in Japan and the U.S. His works *Bali Entranced, Bali: The Island of Festivals and Performers* and *Bali: The Demonic, the Godly and the Wonderous* have received international acclaim.

James A. Sugar
American/Mill Valley, California
A certified scuba diver who also holds a commercial pilot's license, Sugar has been a full-time contract photographer for *National Geographic* since 1969. A former NPPA Magazine Photographer of the Year, he has taught photographic workshops at Center of the Eye in Aspen and had a one-man exhibition at the Nikon Gallery in New York.

Barry Sundermeier
American/Los Angeles, California
Sundermeier is a freelance photographer/photo editor who also works for *People* magazine. Previously he worked with Sygma and was the photo editor for Cannon and DeLaurentiis Films, creating the photo stills department for both studios. He also served as an assignment editor on *A Day in the Life of California.*

Patrick Tehan
American/Santa Ana, California
A photo published in *A Day in the Life of America* earned Tehan top honors in the magazine division of the National Press Photographers Association's Picture of the Year competition. In 1981 he was named a Regional Photographer of the Year, and currently is on the photographic staff of the *Orange County Register.*

Jerry Valente
American/New York, New York
Valente has undertaken corporate and editorial assignments for *Newsweek, Fortune* and the New York Stock Exchange. A specialist in hotel advertising, he is a veteran of three previous *Day in the Life* projects.

Steve Vidler
British/Tokyo, Japan
Vidler travels 12 months of the year shooting photographs for leading airline and travel companies.

Dan White   Kansas City 1987

Dan White
American/Kansas City, Missouri
Born in Michigan and educated at the University of Missouri, White worked for several newspapers before forming White & Associates. He works for many major magazines and corporations, and has published a book called *Independence.*

Joy Wolf
American/Santa Monica, California
A freelance photographer since 1985, Wolf began her career with the *Arizona Daily Star* and the *San Jose Mercury News.* She has traveled to Mexico, India and the Philippines on assignment for publications such as *Time, U.S. News & World Report,* the *New York Times* and *People.* Her previous journeys with the *Day in the Life* team have taken her to Japan and throughout America.

Wendy Lane
Dave Langerman
Marilyn LaRocque
Dave Larsen
Tommy Lasorda
Ron Laub
John Lauren
Therese Leary
Joe LeBue
Suzanne Lecock
Yia Lee & Family
Gary Leffew
Jim Leonard
Andrew Levey
Martin Levin
Dianne Levy
John & Eleanor Lewallen
Joe Leward
Jeff Lewelling
William Lewis
Ted Lewis
Ken Lieberman
Leslie Anne Liedtka
Lili Lim
Bill Lindstead
Judy Litner
Barbara Little
Diana, John & Jenna Little
Tom & Susan Lloyd
Edward & Anne Lloyd
Sgt. Locati
Jim/Loftus
Sr. Lombardo
Eric Long
Bill Longly
Roanne Loo
Linda Sue Lord
Barbara Loren
Jerry Loring
Bill Lovejoy
Patti Lucas
Tim Lundeen
Michael Lupardo
David Lyman
Deputy John Lynde
Kelly Lyon
Tracy Lyon
Sally MacCartee
Peggy MacClean
Monica Macia
Janet MacInnis
Captain Dennis Madigan
Diedre Madsen
Judi Magann
Sheilah Maher
Francis Mahoney
Ken Maley
Kathleen Maloney
Noli Manas
Alfred Mandel
Peter Mann
Ron Mann
Thom Marchionna
Bill Markovich
Carlos Marquez-Sterling
Kimberly Ann Marsh
Elizabeth Marshall
Mike Marshall
Mike Martin
Terrence Martin
Dominic Martin
Jeannee Martin
Ana Martinez
Hilbert Martinez
Paul Marvelly
Amy Masuda
Lela Matheny
Lucienne & Richard
  Matthews
Mike Mattos
Deik Maxwell
Alezine & Clem Mayes
Mike & Martha Mazzaschi
Carol McArthur
Holloway McCandless
Tom McConnel
Father Daniel McCotter
James McCulla
Bob McDermott
Helen McDonald
John McDonough
Mayor Tom McEnery
Cathy, Heather & Louie
  McFarlin

John B. McGlade
Mike McGowen
Paul McGuire
Florian McGuire Moore
Brian McInerney
Barbara McKay
Kristen McKillop
Paul McNally
Michele McNally
Chief Joseph McNamara
Barbara Mecca
Nick Melas
Deborah Mendenhall
Sister Andrea Mendoza
Sgt. Dwight Messimer
Galen Metz
Bob Middleton
Johnny Milano
Thomas H. Miller
Pam Miller
Melanie Miller
Alan Miller
Ron Miller
Henrey & Mabel Miller
Margaret Ann
  Miller-Williams
Ida Mintz
Carol Mir
Pam Miracle
Nancy Miscia
Major Tom Mitchell
Phillip Moffitt
Aileen Moffitt
Robert Mohl
Annie Moller-Rackoe
Arthur Mont
Hank Montgomery
Fred Moore
Alison Morley
Ann Moscicki
Sue Moss
Bruce Mowery
Mary Moyers
Karen Mullarkey
Barbara Murphey
Roger Murphy
Stephen Murphy
Lon Murphy
Jack Murphy
Micheal Mylie
Julia Nagano
Mike Naimark
Kevin Nance
Claude Nederovique
David Neilsen
Steve Nelson
Phil Nelson
Jason Ness
Klaus Neumann
Sue Neumeier
Terry Nicastro
Mike Nicely
Rochelle Nicholas
Nick Nishida
Wendy Nobil
Douglas Norby
Barbara Norman
Kerri Norquist
Al Norris
Chuck Novak
Ruthie Nye
Chris O'Riley
Dan O'Shea
Jim Oberg
Rich Odell
Arthur Ollman
Nancy Olmstead
Kari Olson
Adam Osborne
Gene Ostroff
Conan David Owen
Marganne & David Oxley
Sondra Ozolins
David Pacheco
Lou Pacioco
Mary Page
Elizabeth Anne Palladino
Rusty Pallas
Darlene Papalini
Rick Pappas
Tim Parsons
Jackie Pate
Fritz Paulus
Kathy Paver

Kent Payne
Robert Paz
Reginald Pearman
Susan Pedersen
Steven Peer
Greg Pell
Charles Pellerin
Lynn Penny
Tyler Peppel
Steve, Barbara & Amy
  Pereira
Elizabeth Perle
Susan Peters
Don Peters
Jeff Peterson
Larry Peterson
Lori Peterson
Patrick & Tanya Phillips
Lance M. Pierson
Jeff Piety
Roger Pisani
Carl Pite
Andy Pleasant
Catherine Pledge
Robert Pledge
John Poimiroo
Harry Polatsek
Cliff Polland
Elena Portalupi
Alison Portello
Catherine Porter
Carmen Posada Moreno
Bill Post
Courtney & Harriet
  Proctor
Darcy Provo
Eleanor Prugh
Paul Pruneau
Jeff Pruss
Michael Putnam
Cherie Quaintance
Liz Quick
Robert Rabkin
Eric Raman
Raji Raman
Phil Ramey
Michael Rand
Major Suzanne Randle
Alan Randle
Vicki Raucci
Charles Redmond
Gary Reed
Monty & Barbara Reed
Pamela Reed
Reggie Reese
Barbara Regan
Jim Reichardt
Spencer Reiss
Dale Rennie
Dave Repp
Georgia Ressmeyer
Joe & Ruth Ressmeyer
Jerry Reznick
Scott Rice
Thomas P. Rielly
Ron Riesterer
Brenda Rigby
J.M. Ritter
Ann Rizzo
Jan Robbins
L.G. Roberts
Sid Robinson
John Robinson
Daniel Robuck
Jim Roehrig
Phil Rollins
Cal Romias
Dick Roodzant
John Rosales
K.C. Rosenberg
Mike, Carole & Molly
  Rosenfeld
Josh Rosenfeld
Michael Rosenkrantz
Mike Ross
Bob Roth
Judith Rowcliffe
Jan Rowley
Peter Royce
Heng Ru
Dr. Abraham Rudolph
Jeff Russell
Joe Russo
Burt Rutan

Pat Ryan
Tom Ryder
Mark Rykoff
Joseph Saavedra
Dan Sabovitch
Barbara Sadick
Nola Safro
Hiroshi Sagara
Janet Sakhuja
Sanjay Sakhuja
Ramiro Salcedo
Ernie Salgado
Marcellas Salinas
Bill Salmon
Marianne Samenko
Bill Samenko
Curt Sanburn
Sylvia Sanders
Susan Sanford
Fred Santana
Debra Sass
Gilbert Saucedo
Anthony Scaturro
Steve Schaffran
Cathy Scheidt
Steve Scheier
Hal Schell
Fred Scherrer
Jennifer Schlentz
Ricky Schlessinger
Hank Schnel
Mary Jane Schramm
Mitchel Schrier
Steve Schwartz
Dr. Leonard & Millie
  Schwartz
Rusty Schwimmer
Leonard Sclafani
John Scully
Al Seib
Tom Sellars
Jim Sexton
Scott Shafer
Neil & Karen Shakery
Doug Shane
Ruth Shari
Kerry Shearer
William Sheehan
Brian Sheehy
Captain Sherman
Eleanor Sherman
Elizabeth Davis Sherman
Steven & Danan Sherman
Raj Sheth
Dennis Shinn
Judith Shmueli
Ralph Shock
Rob Shore
Sgt. Virgil Short
Timpisha Shoshone
David Shultz
Laura Shultz
Judith Shunwell
Michael Shure
Bob Sibilia
Frank Sikes
Arlene Silk
Mitch Silverberg
Gene Silverman
Roland & Luenda Silvestri
Mark Simon
Bob Sims
Andrew Singer
Joe Singletary
Bob Siroka
Victoria Sirota
Kerry Skeen
Jay Slattery
Doug Sleeter
Grace Slick
Burrell Smith
Doug Smith
Temple Smith
Richard M. Smith
Roger Smith
Greg Smith
David Smith
Larry Smith
Wayne Smith
Marvin & Gloria Smolan
Leslie & Sandy Smolan
Jo Ann Snyder
Joy & Marty Solomon
Roberto Soningerametta

Ed Sousa
Sam Spear
Phil Sperr
Karen Spotloe
Donald Stang
Diane Stanley
Lane Starling
Dennison Steck
Ann Marie Stein
Bill Stein
Boh Stein
Mitch Stein
Randi Steinman
Captain Stephenson
Michele Stephenson
Tanya Sterling
Gary Sterling
Jim Stevens
Sue Stevens
Andy Stewart
Olivia Stewart
Shannon Stewart
Ray & Lanie Stewart
Jack Stewart
Tom Stillman
Marian Stilz
Kurt Stocker
Jim Stockton
Kevan & Dave Stodd
Jesse Stoery
Eric Stoltz
Michael Story
Igor & Dorothy
  Stowbunenko
Viraj & Daniel
  Stowbunenko
Vince Streano
Blanche Streeter
Lillian Strobel
Dick Stum
Peter & Kristy Sturges
Michele Stuzen
Francisco Suarez
Jan Zahler Sugar
Lydia Sullivan
Debbie Sundahl
R.C. Sutaria
Peter Sutch
Eric Swain
Charleigh Swanson
Ken Swartz
Rick Swig
Martin Swig
Frank Sykes
Joan Tabernik
Barbara Talvola
Jon Tandler
Jay Tannenbaum
Michael Tchao
Elizabeth Terwilliger
Lisa Thackaberry
Billy Thomas
Sgt. Larry Thomas
Cathy Thomas
Peggy Thompson
Carol & Chris Thomson
Jordan Thorn
Barbara & David Thurber
George Thurlow
Dan Tichonchuk
Grid Toland
Linda Toliver
Craig Tolman
Barbara Tomicich
Tom Tondee
Tom Toomey
Ed Tourtellotte
Barbara Townsend
Bill Tracy
June Tran
Janet Trefethen
Harold Trimmer
Jeanne Trombly
Sharon Truax
Mike Tsarnas
Karen Tucker
Jerry & Nadine Tugel
Ross Turner
Robert Ugsang
Russ Underwood
Judy Valenzuela
Charlene Valeri
Della Van Heyst
Vea Van Kessel

Lou Varga
Bill Vela
Ignacio Vella
Sindee Ventre
David Vertin
Pam Vessey
Laurie Vietti
Lydia Villaarreal
Janice Vink
Linda Vivian
Therese Vu
David Vurton & Gail Davis
Pat Walker
Tom Walker
John Walston
Tom Walters
Vince Wang
Gerald Ward Jr.
Larry Warner
John Warnock
Charlene Warr
Bob Warren
Dotia Warrington
Vikki Wartner
Christina Waters
Jeanine Marie Wathen
Ray Watts
Glen Weaver
Jeannette Webber
Michael Weber
Marlene & Robb Weibel
Peter Weinberger
Joan Weiser
Father Michael Weishaar
Allan Weiss
Donna Wells
Lacy Wells
Bob Werner
Jerry Westenhaver
Marty Weybret
Eric & Lael Weyenberg
Karen White
Stephanie Whitmont
Dave Willard
Mike Williams
Julie Williams
Marshall Williams
Dennis Williams
Michael Williamson
Susan Wilson
Mayor Lionel Wilson
Carol Wilson
Dave Winer
Peter Winer
Matt Winokur
Mark Winslow
Danny Wiss
Paul Witteman
Stephen Wolf
Carolyn Wolf
Don Woodley
Jimmy Woods
Susan Woodward
Peter & Carolan Workman
Simon Worrin
Janet Wrather
Lewis Wright
Mary Ann Wright
Hank Wright
Bill Wright
Tom Wrubel
Corky Wykoff
Larry & Linda Wyner
Amy Yamasake
James Yates
Jean Yee
Mike & Dorothea
  Yuschenkoff
Loki & Mark Yuschenkoff
Michael, Chris & Sierra
  Zanger
Cliff Zelman
Esperanza Zendejas
Heidi Zimmerman
Julie Zirbel
Fran Zone
Ed Zwick

And special thanks to Ray
DeMoulin, George Craig
and Sonia Land

James A. Sugar

Sponsors and Contributors

Sponsors
Eastman Kodak Company
BankAmerica Corporation
Hyatt Regency San Francisco
United Airlines
MCI Telecommunications
  Corporation
California Department of
  Commerce
Hertz

Major Contributors
Abaton
Aerolineas Argentinas
Air France
Apple Computer, Inc.
Barneyscan Corporation
Blue & Gold Fleet
British Airways
California Tourism
  Corporation
Eagle Creek Travel Gear
Farallon Computing, Inc.
George Rice & Sons
Iberia, Airlines of Spain
Marriott Corporation
Mexicana Airlines
Pallas Photo Lab, Inc., Denver
Pier 39
Plantronics, Inc.
Professional Photo Repair Inc.
  of San Francisco
SuperMac Technology
Symantec's Living Videotext
  Division
Symantec's THINK
  Technologies Division
The Wine Institute
United Express
WestAir Airlines

Contributors
A Rainbow at Dawn
Adobe Systems
Americoach, Charter Dept.
Artisan Wines
Avis, Cresent City
Avis, Mammoth Lakes
Avis, Medford, Oregon
Beale AFB Public Relations
Bedford Hotel, San Francisco
Beringer Vineyards
Best Western Parkside Inn,
  Fresno
Best Western Peppertree Inn,
  Santa Barbara
Best Western Yosemite
  Way Station, Mariposa
Beverly Garland Hotel,
  North Hollywood
Biltmore Hotel, Los Angeles
Blue Chip Cookies
Bold Flying Service
Bouchaine Vineyards
Breakers Motel of Morro Bay
Cable Car Charters
California Employment
  Development Dept.
Callaway Vineyard & Winery
Captain Dillingham's Inn,
  Benicia
Carneros Creek Winery
Cedar Creek Farms
Chalk Hill Winery

The Chamber of Commerce,
of the following cities
  Bakersfield
  Chico
  Eureka
  Livermore
  Los Angeles
  Modesto
  Oakland
  San Diego
  San Francisco
  San Luis Obispo
  San Pedro
  Santa Barbara
  Santa Maria
  Santa Rosa
  Temecula
  Vallejo
Cherry Hill Travel, Denver
Christian Brothers
Clos du Val Wine Company
Coming Home Hospice
Conestoga Hotel
Country Squire Inn, Auburn
Downtowner Inn, Bakersfield
Eagle House, Eureka
El Dorado School,
  Visitation Valley
Fetzer Vineyards
Frog's Rentacomputer
Furnace Creek Ranch,
  Death Valley
Geyser Peak Winery
Gondola Getaway,
  Long Beach
Grand House Restaurant
  & Cottages, San Pedro
Grosvenor House,
  San Francisco
Heitz Wine Cellars
Holiday Inn, Livermore
Holiday Inn, Modesto
Hyatt Regency Oakland
Hyatt Regency Long Beach
Hyatt Regency Sacramento
Hyatt San Jose Airport
Jukebox Saturday Night,
  San Francisco
Krishna Copy Center
KRON, Telecopter-4

Livingston & Company
Los Robles Lodge, Santa Rosa
M/V Productions
MacToday
MacWeek
Marriott Airport, Los Angeles
Marriott Airporter,
  Burlingame
Marriott Berkeley Marina
Marriott Downtown,
  San Diego
Marriott Rancho Las Palmas
  Resort
Martin Brothers Winery
Matador Motel, Chico
Memorial Medical Center,
  Long Beach
Microsoft Corporation
Moniterm
Monticello Inn, San Francisco
Mousetrak Systems
Otter Bar Lodge
Park Motel, Tulelake
Personal Training Systems
Photographic Center of
  the Monterey Peninsula
Prescott Elementary School
  Clown Troop
Primal Screen
Quality Suites, San Luis
  Obispo
Radius, Inc.

Rancho California Inn,
  Temecula
Raymond Vineyard &
  Cellar, Inc.
Rutherford Hill Winery
San Diego Metro Transit
  Development Board
San Diego Princess Resort
San Francisco Alive
San Francisco Convention &
  Visitors Bureau
San Francisco Symphony
  Orchestra
San Luis Garbage Co.
Santa Maria Inn, Santa Maria
Seghesio Wineries
Shasta Mountain Guides
Skylark Motel, Lakeport
Sony Corporation of America
State of California Dept.
  of Parks & Recreation
T-Bear
Thacher School
The Bay Club
The Hill House of
  Cabot Cove
The Maternity Nurses of
  Memorial Medical Center,
  Long Beach
The Queen Mary
The Yeagar Guest House
Thums, Long Beach
Town House Motel,
  Marysville
Trefethen Vineyards
Two Rock Coast Guard
  Training Center
U.S. Naval Station,
  Long Beach
Villa Florence Hotel,
  San Francisco
Vintage Court, San Francisco
Women's Refuge Center,
  Oakland

Galen Rowell